First published in 2016 by Beatnik Publishing.

A catalogue record for this book is available from the
National Library of New Zealand.

Copyright © 2016 Beatnik Publishing

Text: © Olivia Scott 2016
Photography: © Sally Greer 2016

Design, Typesetting & Cover: © 2016 Beatnik Publishing
Art Direction: Sally Greer
Design: Kitki Tong & Kyle Ranudo

The moral rights of the author have been asserted.

All rights reserved. No part of this publication may be
reproduced or transmitted in any form or by any means,
electronic or mechanical, including photocopying,
recording, or any information storage and retrieval system,
without permission in writing from the publisher.

Printed and bound in China.

ISBN 978-0-9941205-2-6

Beatnik Publishing

PO Box 8276, Symonds Street,
Auckland 1150, New Zealand

www.beatnikpublishing.com

THE
RAW
KITCHEN

OLIVIA SCOTT

CONTENTS

CONTENTS

INTRODUCTION

WHY RAW?

Such is the power of raw and living foods when used as medicine as well as food. – Karen Knowler

Pure, untouched, plant-based food that is not heated over 48°C (117°F) is considered raw food. Raw food includes fresh fruit, vegetables, nuts, seeds, seaweeds and sprouted grains. Raw food has all its pure vitamins, minerals, antioxidants, enzymes, water, oxygen and life force intact – the exact things that enabled the food to grow in the ground in the first place! Your body needs these enzymes to help initiate chemical reactions, such as the production of energy and detoxification of systems. The more enzymes in your body, the more energy you'll have and the faster you'll be able to heal. Our vital functions rely on these enzymes and in many chronic illnesses a decrease of enzyme action is reported, meaning it is especially important to increase enzymes during times of illness. Raw food offers nutritional benefits that cooked food cannot provide, due to losing most of the goodness through heat, which denatures the enzymes and evaporates the water and oxygen content. Cooked food is great too, and definitely has its benefits at times. However, it is through dabbling in raw food that you begin to understand the benefits experienced by increasing your intake of raw.

Over generations, the introduction of antibiotics, processed and pasteurised foods, pesticides, toxins and stress have caused our inner ecosystems to become imbalanced and unhealthy. This damage to our ecosystems can cause poor health, fatigue, depression, obesity and digestive issues. It is becoming more important to take extra care of our bodies, as they become increasingly undernourished. Our bodies replenish cells and blood with nutrients from the food we eat, and by nourishing our ecosystems with raw food, we are giving our bodies the opportunity to create cleaner and more nourished cells that have not been tampered with.

Whether you introduce a raw meal a day, participate in our one-week detox plan or steer down a path of living predominantly raw, you will experience your body shifting gear and you will begin to look and feel more alive and radiant. While we don't advocate starting a long-term 100 percent raw food diet without consulting your health practitioner first, we know that your doctor won't disagree with the benefits of increasing your fruit and vegetable intake!

Benefits of increasing your raw food intake may include:

- increased hydration due to the water content in raw food, giving you fresher and younger-looking skin, shinier hair and sparkly eyes
- increased energy levels
- increased clarity, focus and stamina
- improved digestion
- feeling and looking younger
- cravings for bad foods disappearing
- feeling more harmonious with your body, thoughts and feelings
- a newfound love for life
- a rejuvenated body
- recovering from serious illness or disease, according to some people's reports
- spiritual discoveries of mind and body
- a significant drop in the risk of developing heart and cardiovascular diseases
- alleviation of headaches
- alleviation of allergies
- a boosted immune system
- boosted mental function and memory
- alleviation of arthritis symptoms

MY JOURNEY

The most important thing about eating food is that it should be fun. Food is provided by Mother Nature for us to enjoy and we should eat whatever it is that makes us feel energised, nourished and happy.

Growing up it was expected that I helped out my family in the kitchen. My mum and dad both loved to make food. My mum would make pasta and bread from scratch, and Dad would make pizza, curries and stir-fries. For my fifth birthday I asked my parents for a jar of olives and for my ninth birthday I asked for a big salad with lots of strawberries, pickled onions and balsamic vinegar. I had a unique interest in food from a young age, but the biggest influence on healthy food came from Granny Ann. Granny Ann and her husband Albie built a house on Rakino Island, a small island in the Hauraki Gulf of Auckland, New Zealand, which had no shops, dirt roads and about 20 residents. Her house ran off solar panels, she relied solely on produce from her own garden and eggs from her chickens, and her neighbour would regularly bring them fish caught off the rocks. I spent most of my holidays there and Granny Ann would teach me about the healing powers of flowers, herbs and plants. She would read me tarot cards, we would bake in her kitchen and we would swim in the sea every day. I never knew how much this time with her would later influence and shape my passion for food and wellness. She passed away when I was in my late teens, and that's when my journey began.

Soon after I turned 20, I decided to eat only raw, plant-based foods. I cut out all meat, dairy, refined sugars, refined carbohydrates and processed foods and lived purely off uncooked plant foods. I was beginning my third year as a university student living in the windy and cold city of Wellington, New Zealand. My new diet was an unexpected change in lifestyle for my friends and family, to say the least.

I can't put my finger on exactly what shaped my decision to change my eating, especially considering it was during a time when I was partying, sleeping in, drinking coffee to keep my energy levels up and eating sugary treats to get me through my afternoon lectures. I had never been a fitness or health fanatic; my perception of 'healthy' was two Weetbix with milk for breakfast, a chicken sandwich for lunch and pesto pasta for dinner. I wasn't unhealthy; I didn't feel awful; I just didn't really know (like most people) what was true about nutrition. My life came to a point — it was almost as if a lightbulb switched on — when I knew that I wanted to change my lifestyle in an extreme way. I wanted to change everything, to question all that I knew about food and health, to research further into how to feel better, look better, be the healthiest person I could be in mind and body. I slowly began to realise that there was a huge relationship between the food I put into my mouth and my emotions and relationships with people.

I stripped back everything and went back to basics. As well as changing my diet, I started meditation and yoga and researched quantum physics, the law of attraction and the relationship between nutrition, bacteria and the brain. It all fascinated me, to the point where I would study it late into the night and during my university lectures! Meditation changed my perspective on everything, especially my relationship with myself, which changed the food I wanted to put into my body. The more I changed what I ate, the less I craved bad foods, and the more fresh, green and nutrient-dense foods my body yearned for. One of the most important things I realised was that the more gentle you are with yourself, the more you respect what you put into your body.

I had never felt so alive as during those two-and-a-half years; I felt enlightened and experienced so much clarity. I was able to wake up with boundless amounts of energy and complete essays in a day that would usually take weeks, and took up daily long-distance running to burn off the abundance of new-found energy I had!

At that time, there wasn't much around for raw vegans to eat in Wellington, so I was generally confined to the amenities in my flat: a chopping board, a knife and my flatmate's smoothie blender. This meant big salads and green smoothies were my go-to. I didn't have any fancy equipment, like a spiraliser, dehydrator, or high-speed blender — not even a food processor! I didn't yet know half of what was possible in the raw food world. When I moved back to Auckland, my real journey with raw food began. I enrolled in a holistic nutrition school and got a job at a local raw smoothie bar. I began to get excited about the possibility of this raw food journey when I realised there were other people interested in raw food too. The day I found out there was a local café, Wise Cicada, that sold raw cakes, I think I went and tried every single one there! It really was love at first sight, experiencing these sweet treats after not thinking it was possible to enjoy cakes on a raw food diet.

I was so inspired by the possibilities of raw cakes and my mind began spinning with new flavours and techniques I was dying to try in the kitchen. I decided to spend every last penny I had on ordering a three-kilogram bag of organic cashew nuts, almonds, sunflower seeds and a domestic blender — and got lost in my little kitchen. I would spend my days at nutrition school dreaming of what cakes I would make that night. I would pick up ingredients on my way home and spend evenings with my blender, whipping up cakes, slices and balls. It was this spark of inspiration that brought about The Raw Kitchen.

THE RAW KITCHEN

The business started as an outlet to pour my passion and creativity into. I wanted to create a brand that was accessible to the modern-day person who was interested in food and health. I also wanted to create food that looked and tasted *really good*.

There were a few speed bumps when I started my business, as there always are. I was flatting in a small apartment near Karangahape Road at the time, my method of transport was a bike and I was a full-time student, working weekends at the smoothie bar. I was lucky enough to find a local café called Honeytrap, owned by two sisters, who lent me their café in the evenings in exchange for a jar of Bliss Balls every week. This was the most generous thing anyone could have done to help me get my business started.

I started an Instagram account and posted a couple of pictures of raw cakes. My first one was a beetroot, cacao and ginger tart. A few weeks later I launched a website with the help of my sister. I put ten raw cakes on the website, available to purchase, and waited.

It was about two weeks until my first order came in. I was terrified! It took me three hours to perfect it. I bought the most expensive cake box from the local gift shop, tied it in ribbon, bought flowers for it and the customer came to collect it from my work. Phew! First customer down – would I get a second one?

From there, the cake orders began to flow. I spent most evenings in the little café on K Road, and I started supplying wholesale cakes to cafés around Auckland, after being approached by a woman who owned a café in Epsom.

About eight months in, the business was stocking about twenty-five cafés with raw cakes and balls, and people were ordering cakes nationwide. I found a bigger kitchen, bought a delivery car to replace my bike, and hired my first online assistant (Tori) and kitchen assistant (Alex).

Time flew very quickly and, before we knew it, we were a full-time cake kitchen! We started to sell balls, slices and treats, and we started running workshops for people interested in learning about raw cakes. I stopped studying for my nutrition diploma.

I was lucky that, during this time, the raw food movement had become much bigger. During the first year of running my business, the concept of raw cakes had become almost well known. I put a lot of The Raw Kitchen's quick growth down to social media. I put a lot of time into taking beautiful pictures of the products. Instagram and Facebook played a huge role in getting our name out there and continues to do so; with over 30,000 followers, it is the most effective way of communicating, interacting with and listening to our customers.

The business was two years old when I began looking for a bigger space to open a café. When I met Joss, my partner, he was an owner of seven busy Auckland cafés — and he wanted to help me achieve my dream of running a raw food café. When we stumbled across a beautiful character space on Ponsonby Road, I knew it was perfect: a small shop with a big kitchen and room for classes upstairs.

Joss and I worked hard throughout December 2014 to open the café in January 2015. We hired an amazing front of house team to work in the shop, who were (and still are) as passionate about wellness and food as I am. The Raw Kitchen opened on 15 January and the shop quickly became a humming, happy place with a busy flow of regular customers.

The café has now been running for a year and I still get excited walking into the shop. I still get butterflies thinking I get to do what I love, make food and work with the best team of people. I am most grounded and happy when I am in the kitchen, being creative and bouncing off other people's energy.

Back in university, when I adopted this new way of living, I would never have believed my life would change so quickly and in such a huge way. I feel that I am living my dream and every day I'm immensely grateful for my journey and for whatever it is that changed my direction so abruptly way back then. The crazy journey wouldn't have started if I didn't choose to wake up and take control of my life. Meditation, yoga and diet have all played into the business and into my personal growth and success.

My greater goal, beyond running a wellness brand, is to help people be happier and take charge of their lives in a positive way. Having the opportunity to help others forms part of a greater purpose, of a movement towards a healthier, more conscious world. Whether someone comes into the café only once, visits our blog only once or has a look at our Instagram account only once, if we are able to inspire or motivate that person, then our job is done. It is about sharing passion, creativity and love.

I have created this book for two reasons: firstly, I want to show you how easy it is to create healthy and delicious food at home; secondly, I want you to feel as amazing as nature designed you to feel and realise the importance of food's effect on your mind, body and soul.

RAW FOOD 101: GETTING STARTED

When I began my raw food journey I didn't own a high-speed blender or a food processor. You can make most salads with only a chopping board and a knife, but for many of the other recipes you will need a high-speed blender, a food processor and a dehydrator.

HIGH-SPEED BLENDER

High-speed blenders use immense power to blend ingredients into a smooth paste or liquid. They are great for creating smoothies, sauces, cheesecake fillings and caramel, and grinding nuts into butter. They are a big investment, so make sure you take your time to do some research into what brands are best and what you can afford. After trying a large range of blenders, I can recommend Blendtec and Vitamix; we use both in the café every day in the kitchen and front of house and I wouldn't use anything else.

FOOD PROCESSOR

A food processor is great for blending larger mixtures that do not need to be smooth. For the recipes in this book, I only use the S-blade. The food processor is helpful for creating chunky textures.

DEHYDRATOR

I love using the dehydrator; it is an amazing way of slowly drying foods without damaging the enzymes or nutrient content. I use the dehydrator almost every day to dry tomatoes, fruits, kale chips, crackers, tart cases, vegetables and so much more. It is amazing what you can create and the flavours you can find through drying. Don't forget to always line a dehydrator tray with baking paper.

Raw food isn't heated over 48°C, so I set my dehydrator at 48°C and leave it at that at all times. All recipes in this book that call for the dehydrator are to be set at 48°C.

There are many dehydrators available and I have tried many different types. The most versatile I have used are square dehydrators with trays that you are able to slide in and out. These are the easiest to create raw dishes with (as opposed to circular or fixed-tray dehydrators). It is easier to make crackers on square trays and you can put larger items such as bread tins or cake bases inside without any trouble. If you are looking at purchasing a dehydrator I can recommend Sedona or Excalibur.

SPIRALISER

I put zucchinis, carrots, beetroots and parsnips through a spiraliser to create noodles for dishes such as Pad Thai and Spaghetti Bolognaise. Spiralisers are fairly cheap and are great fun to use with the kids. Most wholefood stores sell spiralisers; otherwise, you can source them online

ORGANIC PRODUCE

While I advocate using organic produce where you can, it is okay if you cannot find organic. Eating organic food is a priority for me at home; however, I don't stress if I can't find what I need. In the café, we aim to be organic when we can and work with our produce suppliers to source organic where possible, but we don't advertise or promote this. This is because I would prefer to deliver delicious food that is organic most of the time than to overcommit to being 100 percent organic and not be able to reach that goal. I absolutely believe that supporting your local growers and growing your own vegetables is the best way to eat.

Some fruits and vegetables are more likely to absorb pesticides and chemicals than others. The most important produce to find organic is:
Apples, Capsicum, Celery, Cherries, Grapes, Lettuce, Nectarines, Peaches, Pears, Potatoes, Spinach

The least contaminated produce is usually:
Asparagus, Avocados, Bananas, Broccoli, Cabbage, Corn, Kiwifruit, Mango, Onions, Papaya, Peas, Pineapples

RAW FOOD 101: INGREDIENTS & THEIR NUTRITIONAL BENEFITS

Once I began to start investing in my health, my body gave back to me an abundance of energy, vitality, good skin and immunity. When you start using good-quality produce, nuts, herbs and superfoods as ways of investing in your body, your perspective shifts as you begin to see the positive changes.

One of the ways you can start a healthier you is giving your pantry an overhaul! Throw away anything that you no longer want to eat and introduce healthier options or substitutes. Once you feel organised, you will be energised to get creative in the kitchen and prepare healthy meals for youself and your friends and family. Preparation is key with plant-based foods. Once you have everything at your fingertips, you will find it easy to throw recipes together.

Below are some common ingredients used in this cookbook and their nutritional benefits.

Agave nectar/syrup is occasionally used in the café to sweeten desserts that need a sharp flavour. While I don't usually advocate using agave nectar because of its high fructose content, it really does offer a clean sweetness that can make the most delicious dessert pop. It is not the gentlest sweetener, but if used in moderation it is excellent. I recommend reading further into agave nectar and finding out whether it will work for you.

Almonds are chock-a-block with omega-3s, antioxidants, magnesium, zinc and more. They also provide a hit of protein and healthy fats to make for a nutritionally complete milk option.

Almond mylk is a great staple to have on hand. I use almond mylk every day at home in my hot drinks, smoothies and muesli. You can purchase organic almond mylk from most supermarkets or wholefood stores, or you can make your own (check out my recipe on page 234).

Apple cider vinegar is another favourite of mine as it adds a zestiness to savoury foods. Apple cider vinegar is great for aiding digestion; it is full of beneficial bacteria and enzymes. Not only full of health benefits, it can sharpen a flavour, add a kick to salad, add life to a sauce or balance a sweet cheese or cake filling. It's handy to have in the pantry when playing with flavours.

Avocado is a rich source of good fats that help regulate cholesterol levels and promote a healthy heart. This amazing fruit also contains vitamin E, glutathione and carotenoids, making it a super antioxidant.

Bee pollen contains nearly all nutrients required by humans; it's therefore one of nature's most completely nourishing foods. It's richer in protein than any animal source, thus acting as a natural energy booster. It will also support the immune system, and cardiovascular and digestive health.

Black garlic has twice the amount of antioxidants of regular garlic! It gets its chewy texture by being kept in temperature-controlled humidity over the course of 30 days, causing it to slowly caramelise. It is commonly referred to as 'fermented garlic'.

Buckwheat is a wheat- and gluten-free grain. It is a rich source of soluble fibre, which provides a steady and sustained energy release, as well as being satiating and promoting healthy digestion. Soaking buckwheat is important in recipes as it 'activates' the buckwheat, which removes the enzyme-inhibiting layer and begins to germinate the buckwheat seed, bringing it back to life. If the buckwheat continues to be rinsed, it will begin to sprout. However, in all of the recipes in this book that call for soaked buckwheat, the buckwheat simply needs to be 'activated', which is the initial part of this sprouting process. This is done simply by soaking the buckwheat in filtered water for 8 hours and rinsing. This process aids the digestion of the buckwheat and increases the nutritional content as it boosts the enzyme, vitamin and mineral content. Buckwheat is known to be high in B vitamins and a rich protein source.

Cacao is a super antioxidant that boosts brain function and is known to improve overall mood. It is also rich in magnesium, which may help reduce muscle tension and promote restful sleep.

Cacao nibs are raw cacao beans that have been ground into smaller nibs. They are great for decorating and add a beautiful bitterness to raw sweets. I love to roll Bliss Balls in nibs, to add an extra crunch.

Cacao powder is the raw cacao bean ground up into a fine powder. The difference between supermarket 'cocoa' and raw cacao powder is that this hasn't been heated and all nutrients are intact.

Cardamom has long been used to soothe the stomach and intestines, easing digestion and other gastrointestinal issues.

Carob powder is a great substitute for cacao powder if you are sensitive to caffeine. It has a slightly caramel-like flavour and is delicious in raw desserts.

Carrots provide high levels of beta-carotene, which is converted to vitamin A in the body. This promotes healthy eyes, enhanced immunity and overall cell growth and maintenance. Adding carrots and cinnamon to a juice may help to regulate blood sugar levels, which is important for heart health.

Cashews are a must in your raw kitchen! They create beautifully smooth, velvety cheesecakes, cheeses, nut milks and garnishes on salads. I usually soak my cashews for 4–8 hours to help create a smoother texture. They contain a great variety of nutrients that will help regulate blood sugar and lower cholesterol, and may even have cancer-fighting properties. And, of course, cashews are a great source of protein and healthy fats.

Cayenne pepper is something I like to use to bring warmth to dishes, especially raw soups and curries that are served chilled and would usually be warm. Using just a pinch of cayenne pepper can change the dish, so experiment carefully! Cayenne pepper is also great for digestion, as it increases the flow of gastric juices and enzyme production, increases circulation and is also antifungal.

Chamomile acts as an antibacterial that calms and soothes the body.

Chia seeds are powerhouses of nutrition and one of my favourite breakfast ingredients. They are so easy to use when whipping up decadent but healthy breakfasts. These seeds can be considered a complete protein containing all amino acids, as well as omega-3 fatty acids and important minerals such as magnesium, calcium and dietary fibre. These nutrients will help support energy production, bone health and heart health — not to mention leaving you feeling very satisfied!

Cinnamon is a soft, warm spice that gives a unique and satisfying flavour to both sweet and savoury dishes. It helps to wake up your metabolism in the morning and soothe your digestive system. The addition of cinnamon to almond mylk may soothe digestion.

Coconut milk is a great staple to have on hand to use in both sweet and savoury dishes. Look for organic coconut milk and cream, as non-organic may contain thickening agents and preservatives. Alternatively you can make your own by blending the flesh of young coconuts with water.

Coconut oil, extra virgin is a main staple of my pantry; I love it and use it every day. It is a light, delicious oil that helps hold together sweets and gives a fresh, smooth flavour. Make sure you buy the cold-pressed coconut oil, which is in its most pure form. Stay away from deodorised coconut oil, as it is made from the coconut kernels rather than the coconut flesh and does not offer the same health and flavour benefits that extra virgin coconut oil offers. Coconut oil is an antibacterial which is great for both your skin and gut. It is more commonly known for its healthy saturated fat content, which is essential for brain function, a healthy immune system and a healthy metabolism. For the recipes in this book, coconut oil should be melted.

Coconut sugar has a similar flavour to maple syrup and is a gentle, low GI option for sweetening dishes. I often use coconut sugar in desserts that traditionally use brown sugar; for example, apple cobbler. It is great when you want to achieve a subtle crystallised sugar pop in the texture of the dessert. I also love to sprinkle a pinch on top of my bircher muesli or gluten-free oats in the morning. It provides you with a fantastic source of energy due to the immediate ingestion of its medium-chain fatty acids. Some of these fatty acids, such as lauric acid, are antibacterial.

Coconut, dried (desiccated or coconut chips) is best when organic, as quite often sulfur is used to preserve coconut. The flavour is also very different. Coconut is an important staple, as you can very quickly make up a milk or dessert with it.

Coconut, young Thai can be sourced from local markets or from most wholefood stores. The flesh is absolutely divine in desserts, ice cream and yoghurt, or just eaten alone. If you can find these coconuts then definitely use them in your recipes. You will notice a big difference in flavour, quality and consistency.

Dates are commonly used as a sweetener in this book. I use soaked, pitted dates to sweeten a lot of cakes and treats, as I love that they are a wholefood and offer a range of nutrients. Dates are rich in fibre and are full of vitamins and minerals. I still choose dates over most sweeteners, as they also add a beautiful texture to a cake recipe when soaked. Soaking dates is essential for a great texture in sweets. When a recipe

asks for dates to be soaked, 4–8 hours in cold filtered water is best. If you are in a rush, then you can use warm filtered water to speed up the soaking process.

Ginger has anti-inflammatory qualities and helps to improve circulation. It has been widely used to ease indigestion, nausea and other digestive complaints.

Goji berries are loaded with antioxidants and beta-carotene, providing reduced free-radical activity in the body and thus healthy cells. These unique little berries will promote immunity, as well as healthy skin, hair and eyes.

Flaxmeal (ground flaxseeds/linseeds) is often used in my recipes as a binder in dehydrated foods such as bread, pizza bases, crackers and pancakes. When a recipe asks for flaxmeal, you can place flaxseeds/linseeds (same thing) in a spice grinder, mortar and pestle or high-speed blender and grind/blend to get a fine consistency. The consistency is important as it helps to create a smooth texture and releases the gel-like properties that are helpful in binding the ingredients together. Flaxmeal is rich in fibre, and is one of the most beneficial foods for your gut as the soluble fibre helps to clean your digestive tract and remove excess waste.

Hazelnuts are my favourite nut to use, as they have such a unique flavour and team so well with both sweet and savoury dishes. I always have a stash in the pantry so I can use them chopped over salads, in soups, in raw sweets or just to snack on. I also activate hazelnuts to ensure the hazelnut's nutrients are maximised, and so they are digested more easily. For more information on activating nuts, see page 15.

Honey has only recently come onto my radar as a suitable sweetener. Up until this year, I have maintained a vegan-only approach to sweetening food. Of course, honey and bee pollen is not vegan, due to it being an animal product. I have recently started using locally sourced raw honey. When you use honey that is sustainably sourced nearby, your body processes the local pollens in the honey and desensitises to any allergies associated with those pollens.

Irish moss paste is a thickening agent used in cakes, sauces and jams. It is a seaweed that originally comes from Ireland, and is washed, dried and packaged and sent all over the world. I love using Irish moss in my cakes and it is my preferred method of setting cakes. It is light and smooth and gives a cheesecake-like consistency to cakes and slices.

Kefir is a fermented beverage. It provides beneficial bacteria, yeast, vitamins, minerals and complete proteins to the body. It has a cleansing effect that contributes to regular digestion and a healthy immune system. Kefir is very easy to make and is a potent form of probiotics.

Kefir grains are a yeast/bacterial fermentation starter (similar to SCOBYs – see below) that feed off sugars. They create an effervescent drink, due to the fermentation process.

Kombucha is a naturally fermented tea that will act as a probiotic to stimulate your healthy gut bacteria. This will in turn improve your digestive processes and increase your body's ability to utilise important nutrients. A kombucha SCOBY (symbiotic culture of bacteria and yeast) is used to ferment the tea and sugar into a delicious, healthy drink. I have always managed to come across SCOBYs by word of mouth. Once you put it out there that you are looking for a SCOBY you usually hear of a friend who has one you can have. They grow very quickly if you continue to feed them. You can also find SCOBYs at most wholefood shops.

Lavender is a wonderful, soothing flower that may be beneficial for anxiety, depression, indigestion and even colic.

Liquid smoke is a smoked water and can be found in most wholefood stores or online. It can be added to sauces, nut mince, eggplant bacon and dips to add a subtle smokiness, similar to smoked paprika. It is amazing what this condiment can do to a dish – you will love it once you try it!

Lucuma powder is one of my favourite superfoods. It gives recipes an almost milky, white-chocolatey flavour. It is a Peruvian fruit that is dried and blended into a fine powder. It is naturally sweet with a low GI, so is therefore effective in regulating blood sugar and insulin levels.

Maca powder is an amazing superfood that tastes subtly caramel-like with a malty smell. It is a Peruvian root that is dried and blended into a fine powder. I love to use maca sprinkled over breakfasts and in raw desserts to enhance the flavour. Maca powder has long been used for energy, strength and stamina, and may increase energy and endurance by oxygenating the blood.

Macadamias are such indulgent nuts, so full of flavour and creaminess. I only use small amounts of macadamias, as they are very rich in flavour and often expensive. I love adding macadamias to salad dressings, icings and cakes. Soaking is a good option with these nuts to help them blend and give an element of decadence to a cream.

Maple syrup is a beautiful sweetener but it is not raw. Maple syrup is extracted from a maple tree and then heated. I still, however, do use this sweetener occasionally, as it offers benefits that no other sweetener does. When maple syrup is used in recipes such as cookies, wraps and pastry, it creates a pliable and chewy consistency like no other raw ingredient can. It creates that 'brownie-like' chewiness that is so delicious in raw treats. If you are following a strict raw diet, use coconut sugar instead of maple syrup.

Matcha powder is finely ground green tea that has been specially grown and processed. It packs a delicious savoury punch and is absolutely packed full of antioxidants that will help promote healthy cells throughout your entire body, thus minimising symptoms commonly associated with ageing. Matcha is a naturally alkalising and detoxifying choice for your body.

Miso paste I often use in my savoury dishes to add a greater depth of umami. When teamed with other ingredients such as tamari and maple it can create a complexity of flavour that is perfectly balanced for savoury dishes. Miso is rich in antioxidants, giving it anti-aging properties; it is full of beneficial gut bacteria, as well as being abundant in B vitamins, proteins and enzymes.

Nuts and seeds, activated are usually soaked to start the germination process, activating the enzymes in the nut and removing the layer of enzyme inhibitors. This process helps with digestion of the nut, as the digestion inhibiting phytic acid is removed and the nutrition content is increased. After the nuts have soaked and activation process has started, I gently warm them in the dehydrator for 24 hours to remove moisture, which still keeps them in their activated state. They have a unique crunchiness that is beautiful as a garnish, in salads, or in the bases of cakes and slices. I love to marinate nuts in a sauce while dehydrating, and keep them with me in my bag for snacking throughout the day!

Nut butters are great for adding to smoothies, for spreading on toast or celery, or licking straight off the spoon! With a high-speed blender you can even make your own at home and get creative with different nuts. An ABC (almond, brazil nut, cashew) combination will give you an abundance of nutrients and energy.

Nutmeg is a beautiful spice that is best freshly grated. You generally need only a small amount in recipes as it has a strong kick but can create a nostalgic flavour, especially when teamed with chocolate. Nutmeg is great for aiding digestion, improving circulation and helps to stimulate the liver.

Oats, gluten-free are often hard to find, but can be sourced online if you cannot get them from your local health food store. I use gluten-free oats for making pastry and dough as they help to imitate that classic pie or crust texture. Gluten-free oats are also great in bircher muesli and porridge. Oats are incredibly rich in fibre, and many essential vitamins and minerals. Starting your day with a bowl of bircher muesli is an amazing way to flood your body with the energy it needs to run well.

Olive oil, extra virgin is a gorgeous way of lifting salads, sauces and pestos with a smooth and fragrant flavour. Choosing an oil is almost like choosing a good wine. Read about where the olives have come from and choose depending on your preferred flavour and aroma.

Paprika, smoked is a great way of adding a wood-smoky flavour to a raw dish without heating anything. It isn't a raw spice, but I find that using spices like this often helps to bring out the flavours of the raw ingredients. Omit from recipes if you are following a strictly raw diet.

Pineapples contain the amazing proteolytic enzyme known as bromelain, which is a strong anti-inflammatory that will also support protein digestion. They are also rich in vitamin C and are one of the best food sources of manganese, which is important for efficient metabolism of carbohydrates, proteins and cholesterol.

Psyllium husk is a great pantry staple, as it is an effective way to thicken foods. It is a very quick moisture-absorbing food, so is added at the end of most mixtures before pouring. Psyllium comes from the husks of the Plantago ovata plant's seed. It comes in both husk and powder form. I use the powder, but if you can't find this, psyllium husk is great too.

Pumpkin seeds are a favourite of mine to activate, as they plump up and become deliciously crispy when dehydrated. Use organic seeds if you can — the flavour and texture are more vibrant.

Rice malt syrup is my favourite sweetener because of its low fructose content and low glycaemic index rating. It is gentle on the body and the digestive system. It gives desserts a rounded sweetness but doesn't offer the clean sweetness that I sometimes want to achieve with desserts (it often leaves a subtle malt-like flavour — usually only noticed by perfectionists like me). It is great if you don't like your treats super sweet.

Stevia is an extract from the stevia leaf, which has a naturally sweet flavour. Stevia doesn't affect the glycaemic load in the body and is gentler than most sweeteners. I like to add a drop to hot chocolate or in a mousse or chia pudding. It has a unique flavour and, depending on the brand, can sometimes not quite work in recipes due to its aftertaste. I recommend trying it out in small amounts before trying to sweeten a large dessert or pudding.

Sunflower lecithin is the secret to the creaminess of our Almond Mylk. Sunflower lecithin is an extract from the sunflower and is used in foods to bind the water and fat components. It helps to prevent nut mylks from separating, which usually occurs naturally as the fat from the almonds is heavier than the water. Without lecithin, the mylk will need stirring as the fat drifts to the top and the water sits on the bottom. It is also common to use sunflower lecithin in raw cakes, to create a creamier, smoother consistency.

Sunflower seeds are a wonderful pantry staple as they are great in almost anything. I love putting them in cake bases in place of nuts. They are especially great as a nut-free option for those with nut allergies.

Sweeteners are something people often ask me about in relation to my cakes and treats. It is a tricky question because different sweeteners come with different aftertastes which change the flavours of desserts. Throughout the book I suggest different sweeteners for different recipes, but I urge you to try alternative sweeteners to suit your taste and preference.

Tamari is a gluten-free alternative to soy sauce. It adds a beautiful umami savoury flavour to marinades, crackers and dressings.

Turmeric provides an array of nutritional and flavour benefits and can be used in both sweet and savoury meals. The colour is also beautiful. I love to create warm turmeric drinks in the winter and throw it in salads and salad dressings in the summer. It is a versatile spice that I love to have on hand. If you can source fresh turmeric, even better, but dried turmeric is also great. Turmeric is well known for its anti-inflammatory and antioxidant properties; it is excellent in creating a strong immune system. I love to throw fresh turmeric in my smoothies for a superfood boost.

Vanilla bean powder is the seeds scraped out from the insides of a vanilla bean pod then blended to a powder. I often buy vanilla bean powder by the small tub. It is an investment but will last the distance as you need only a pinch to half a teaspoon in most recipes. It changes the flavour of sweet foods immensely.

Walnuts are rich in monounsaturated fats that are important for heart health, cognitive function and a healthy, glowing complexion.

Yoghurt, coconut or cashew is not only delicious but so good for you! Dairy-free yoghurt is great for topping soups, curries or breakfast dishes or on its own with fresh fruit. It is found in most wholefood stores, or you can easily make your own Vanilla Cashew Yoghurt using my recipe on page 244.

RAW FOOD FAQ

Will I lose weight?

Often people do lose weight on raw food diets because of the low calorie content of fruits and vegetables compared to their usual diet of richer food such as pasta, bread, meat, alcohol or soft drinks. Generally people need to eat more on a raw food diet to fill them up – and this is absolutely fine, especially if you are filling up on plenty of fresh vegetables! However, don't forget that some raw foods are dense and higher in calories, such as raw sweeteners, nuts, seeds and coconut. While these foods are rich in vitamins, minerals and antioxidants and gentler on the body and digestion, it is not recommended to eat them in excess. If losing weight is your goal, then it is recommended to follow a diet rich in vegetables, especially leafy greens, sprouts and healthy fats, with moderate exercise (consult your health practitioner). See our detox plan (page 247) for a sustainable way of maintaining a balanced and nourishing diet.

Will I get sufficient iron, protein and B^{12} levels from eating predominantly raw food?

If you are thinking of following a raw food diet it is recommended you see a health practitioner to get suggestions and recommendations for meeting your requirements. Often raw foodists suggest eating nutritional yeast, seaweeds and spirulina for sources of B^{12}. High levels of protein are found in most nuts, seeds, sprouted grains and green vegetables (kale has more protein than beef per gram!). Iron is also found in leafy greens, so loading your green smoothie up with lots of kale, spinach, silverbeet and collard is recommended.

Where can I find the ingredients listed in your recipes?

In this book I have tried to use ingredients that are easy to find. However, there may be some superfoods or condiments that are not available to you locally. A common website I use to source ingredients is iherb.com. It is a great website for all health-related foods.

Is everything in this book raw?

All the fruits, vegetables, nuts, seeds and sprouts are raw. I believe in leaving food in its most natural state in the way nature intended us to have it. Occasionally I use ingredients such as maple syrup, smoked paprika or dried turmeric to boost flavour in the food. These ingredients are not raw but still contain immense health-boosting properties. They are not processed but simply dried or heated to preserve. If you are following a strictly raw diet, I recommend omitting these ingredients from the recipe.

Can I use my oven instead of a dehydrator?

You can set your oven to a very low temperature and heat food until the preferred texture is reached. Oven temperatures are much harder to control (as all ovens are slightly different), and don't forget that it must not exceed 48°C.

Can I heat the food?

Occasionally I do make my soup recipes and heat them on the stove top. I have customers who take home the Pad Thai Salad and lightly fry it with some coconut oil on the stove top. While I do recommend eating this food raw, you can experiment with warming it.

BREAKFAST

BREAKFAST

BANANA & PEANUT BUTTER PUDDING

INGREDIENTS

1 banana
3 Tbsp **peanut butter**
1½ cups (375ml) **coconut milk** or **Almond Mylk** (see page 234)
1 tsp **cinnamon**
5 Tbsp **coconut sugar**
pinch **vanilla bean powder**
½ cup (125ml) **filtered water**
⅓ cup (55g/1.9oz) **chia seeds**
1 Tbsp **cacao nibs**

METHOD

Place banana, peanut butter, your preferred milk, cinnamon, coconut sugar, vanilla bean powder and filtered water in a high-speed blender, and blend on high until smooth.

Place chia seeds in a jar. Pour the blended liquid into the jar over the chia seeds and stir. Make sure there are no lumps of chia seeds at the bottom.

Refrigerate for at least 2 hours to set (I leave mine to set overnight). To serve, sprinkle with cacao nibs.

Serves 2

RHUBARB & VANILLA PUDDING

INGREDIENTS

2 stalks **rhubarb**, plus extra
to garnish
3 Tbsp **lemon juice**
3 Tbsp **coconut sugar**
2 cups (500ml) **Almond Mylk**
(see page 234)
⅓ cup (100g/3.5oz) **rice malt syrup**
1 tsp **cinnamon**
pinch of **vanilla bean powder**
pinch of **Himalayan sea salt**
⅓ cup (55g/1.9oz) **chia seeds**

METHOD

Slice the rhubarb into strips, 2–5cm long. Place in a small bowl and cover with lemon juice and coconut sugar. Using your hands, massage the sugar and lemon juice into the rhubarb, and place on a dehydrator tray for 1 hour.

Place Almond Mylk, rice malt syrup, cinnamon, vanilla bean powder and sea salt in a high-speed blender, and blend until smooth.

Place chia seeds in a jar. Pour the blended liquid into the jar over the chia seeds and stir. Make sure there are no lumps of chia seeds at the bottom. Refrigerate for at least 2 hours to set.

Place the dehydrated rhubarb in the bottom of another jar, and pour chia pudding on top. To serve, garnish with some extra rhubarb.

Serves 2

TROPICAL CHIA PUDDING

INGREDIENTS

1 cup (250ml) **coconut milk**
1 cup (160g/5.6oz) chopped **pineapple**, plus extra to garnish
flesh of 1 **mango**, plus extra to garnish
½ cup (125ml) **filtered water**
⅓ cup (100g/3.5oz) **rice malt syrup**
pinch of **vanilla bean powder**
⅓ cup (55g/1.9oz) **chia seeds**

METHOD

Place coconut milk, pineapple, mango, filtered water, rice malt syrup and vanilla bean powder in a high-speed blender, and blend on high until smooth.

Place chia seeds in a jar. Pour the blended liquid into the jar over the chia seeds and stir. Make sure there are no lumps of chia seeds at the bottom.

Refrigerate for at least 2 hours to set. To serve, garnish with extra pineapple or mango.

Serves 2

BIRCHER MUESLI

INGREDIENTS

¼ cup (25g/0.9oz) walnuts
1½ cups (135g/4.8oz) gluten-free oats
¼ cup (40g/1.4oz) black chia seeds
¼ cup (40g/1.4oz) flaxseeds
¼ cup (35g/1.3oz) pumpkin seeds
¼ cup (35g/1.3oz) sunflower seeds
½ cup (85g/3oz) sultanas
1 cup (250ml) coconut milk
¼ cup (63ml) lemon juice
1 cup (250ml) filtered water
1 cup (150g/5.2oz) grated apple
6 Tbsp Berry Chia Jelly
(see page 39)

METHOD

Roughly chop walnuts and place in a large bowl. Add oats, chia seeds, flaxseeds, pumpkin seeds, sunflower seeds, sultanas, coconut milk, lemon juice and filtered water and stir until well mixed. Make sure there are no chia seeds stuck to the bottom. Cover the bowl and refrigerate overnight (or for at least 6 hours) to set.

When ready to serve, mix in the grated apple and serve in bowls, each top with three tablespoons of Berry Chia Jelly.

Serves 2

CACAO MUESLI

INGREDIENTS

3 cups (495g/17.7oz) buckwheat,
soaked (see page 11)
½ cup (55g/2oz) raw cacao powder
½ tsp Himalayan sea salt
½ cup (50g/1.8oz) dried coconut
chips or desiccated coconut
½ cup (100g/3.5oz) coconut sugar
1 cup (170g/6oz) sultanas
1 cup (135g/4.8oz) cashews

METHOD

Strain the soaked buckwheat and rinse under clean, running water (until
water runs clear). Place in a bowl and mix with the rest of the ingredients.

When the muesli is mixed thoroughly together, place on dehydrator trays
that have been lined with baking paper and dehydrate for 12 hours, or until
it has reached your preferred crunchiness. Store in an airtight container for
up to two weeks.

Makes 6 serves

CACAO BREAKFAST CUP

INGREDIENTS

1 cup (150g/5.3oz) Cacao Muesli
(see above)
6 Tbsp yoghurt
3 Tbsp Berry Chia Jelly
(see page 39)
⅓ cup (45g/1.6oz) fresh berries

METHOD

Place half the Cacao Muesli in a slim glass tumbler. Spoon half the Berry
Chia Jelly on top, then half the yoghurt. Layer the rest of the muesli on
top, followed by the rest of the Berry Chia Jelly, then the rest of the
yoghurt. Top with the fresh berries.

Serves 1

GINGER & GOJI GRANOLA

INGREDIENTS

2 cups (330g/11.8oz) **buckwheat,**
soaked (see page 11)

4 Tbsp **maple syrup**

2 tsp **ground ginger**

1 cup (140g/4.9oz) **pumpkin seeds**

1 cup (140g/4.9oz) **sunflower seeds**

½ cup (120g/4.2oz) **goji berries**

1 Tbsp **white sesame seeds**

1 Tbsp **black sesame seeds**

TO SERVE

2 Tbsp **yoghurt** of your choice

1 cup (250ml) **Almond Mylk**
(see page 234)

METHOD

Strain the soaked buckwheat and rinse under clean, running water (until water runs clear). Place in a bowl, and mix with maple syrup, ground ginger, pumpkin seeds, sunflower seeds, goji berries, and white and black sesame seeds.

When the muesli is mixed thoroughly together, place on dehydrator trays that have been lined with baking paper and dehydrate for 12 hours, or until it has reached your preferred crunchiness. Store in a large airtight jar or container.

To serve, place ⅔ cup of muesli in each bowl and serve with yoghurt and Almond Mylk.

Makes 6 serves

STRAWBERRY DREAM BOWL

INGREDIENTS

1 cup (220g/7.8oz) **frozen strawberries**

2 **bananas**

½ cup (125ml) **Almond Mylk** (see page 234)

½ cup (75g/2.6oz) **Cacao Muesli** (see page 28)

2 Tbsp **cacao nibs**

6 pieces **Caramel Chocolate** (see page 180)

1 tsp **bee pollen**

METHOD

Place strawberries, bananas and Almond Mylk in a high-speed blender. Blend on low until smooth (about 1–2 minutes). Pour into a bowl and serve with Cacao Muesli, cacao nibs, Caramel Chocolate and bee pollen.

Serves 2

TIP

Bulk buy old bananas, peel and freeze.

CHOC-ORANGE MOUSSE WITH POACHED PEAR

INGREDIENTS

POACHED PEAR
1 pear
½ cup (125ml) lemon juice
¼ cup (75g/2.6oz) maple syrup

MOUSSE
flesh of 1 avocado
2 bananas
1 cup (250ml) Almond Mylk
(see page 234)
2 Tbsp cacao powder
2 Tbsp coconut sugar
1 Tbsp coconut oil
pinch of vanilla bean powder
pinch of Himalayan sea salt

GARNISH
2 Tbsp pistachios, chopped
1 Tbsp orange zest

METHOD

To make the poached pear, place lemon juice and maple syrup in a bowl or glass that will also fit the pear. Peel then halve the pear and slice off the bottom. Place in the glass and refrigerate for at least 2 hours to marinate. Ensure the pear is fully immersed in the liquid; if it isn't, add more lemon juice or water.

To make the mousse, place avocado, bananas, Almond Mylk, cacao powder, coconut sugar, coconut oil, vanilla bean powder and sea salt in a blender and blend until smooth. Pour into two small bowls and place pear halves on top. Garnish with a sprinkle of pistachios and/or orange zest.

Serves 2

TIP

Prepare the pear the night before so you can whip up this delicious chocolate mousse for breakfast in no time! The longer the pear soaks, the softer it is the next day.

MAPLE PANNA COTTA

INGREDIENTS

**IRISH MOSS PASTE
(MAKES 2 CUPS)**
1 cup (70g/2.5oz) Irish moss
5 cups (1.25L) filtered water

PANNA COTTA
flesh of 2 young coconuts or
2 cups (270g/9.6oz) cashews,
soaked (see page 12)
1 cup (250ml) filtered water
½ cup (150g/5.3oz) rice malt syrup
½ tsp vanilla bean powder
1 Tbsp lucuma powder
1 Tbsp maca powder
¾ cup (190ml) coconut oil,
softened
⅓ cup (80g/2.8oz) Irish Moss Paste

SALTED MAPLE SAUCE
¼ cup (75g/2.6oz) maple syrup
½ tsp vanilla bean powder
1 tsp Himalayan sea salt

GARNISH
chopped pistachios

METHOD

To make the Irish Moss Paste, soak Irish moss in 3 cups of filtered water for 30 minutes then, using a large sieve, rinse under running tap water to remove debris and sand. Place cleaned Irish moss in a high-speed blender with 2 cups of filtered water and blend on high for 3 minutes, until it has formed a smooth gel. Pour gel into an airtight container and refrigerate to set. Store, refrigerated, for up to two weeks.

To make the panna cotta, place the coconut flesh or cashews, filtered water, rice malt syrup, vanilla bean powder, lucuma powder, maca powder and coconut oil in a high-speed blender, and blend until smooth. Add Irish Moss Paste and blend further until well combined. Pour into four glass tumblers and refrigerate. Allow to set for 6–8 hours for the best texture. Once set, delicately pour the set panna cotta onto a plate to serve.

To make the salted maple sauce, place all ingredients in a high-speed blender and blend until smooth. Pour the sauce over the panna cotta, and garnish with some chopped pistachios.

Serves 4

TIP

Irish moss is a seaweed which you can soak and blend into a gel that acts like gelatin. It creates a light, fluffy texture that is perfect for a panna cotta.

VANILLA MASCARPONE

INGREDIENTS

2 cups (270g/9.6oz) cashews, soaked (see page 12)
1 cup (250ml) coconut cream
½ cup (150g/5.3oz) rice malt syrup
¼ cup (63ml) lemon juice
3 Tbsp coconut oil
1 tsp nutritional yeast
1 Tbsp miso paste
½ tsp Himalayan sea salt
pinch of vanilla bean powder

METHOD

Place all ingredients in a high-speed blender and blend until smooth. Store in an airtight container and keep refrigerated.

Makes 3 cups

TIP

The addition of miso and nutritional yeast to this recipe creates that traditional cheese-like flavour of mascarpone, with a beautiful addition of citrus and sweetness. I also love to spread this mascarpone on toast, with fresh fruit on top.

BERRY CHIA JELLY

INGREDIENTS

2 cups (270g/9.6oz) **berries** of your choice

2½ cups (625ml) **filtered water**

⅓ cup (75g/2.6oz) **rice malt syrup**

1 Tbsp **lemon juice**

¾ cup (120g/4.2oz) **black chia seeds**

METHOD

Place berries, filtered water, rice malt syrup and lemon juice in a blender and blend until smooth. Pour into a bowl and add chia seeds. Stir for 1–2 minutes, until smooth. Pour into a jar and secure lid.

Refrigerate for 4 hours or until the jelly has reached your preferred texture. This will keep, refrigerated, for one week.

Makes 3 cups

TIP

I like to save a few extra whole berries to throw in at the end, for a chunkier jelly. It's especially nice to do this with fresh blueberries or raspberries when in season.

CHOCOLATE PANCAKE STACK

INGREDIENTS

3 bananas

1 cup (125g/4.4oz) dehydrated almond pulp or almond flour

½ cup (55g/2oz) raw cacao powder

2 Tbsp coconut oil

6 Tbsp flaxmeal

½ cup (150g/5.3oz) maple syrup

½ cup (125ml) Almond Mylk (see page 234)

1½ cups (375ml) filtered water

pinch of vanilla bean powder

½ tsp Himalayan sea salt

TO SERVE

1 cup (225g/8oz) Vanilla Mascarpone (see page 38)

2 Tbsp Berry Chia Jelly (see page 39)

⅓ cup (45g/1.6oz) fresh berries

⅓ cup (100g/3.5oz) maple syrup

METHOD

Place all ingredients in a high-speed blender and blend until smooth. Pour the mixture, in 10cm wide circles (about 0.5cm high), onto a dehydrator tray that has been lined with baking paper. Dehydrate for 4 hours, then flip and dehydrate for another 2 hours on the other side. Serve immediately, or refrigerate, covered, until ready to serve.

To serve, place a pancake in the centre of a plate. Dollop Vanilla Mascarpone on top and spread evenly, going right to the edges. Place another pancake on top and continue to spread the mascarpone right to the edges. For the fifth pancake, spread with mascarpone and place a dollop of Berry Chia Jelly on top, and garnish with fresh berries. Drizzle with maple syrup.

Make the second pancake stack and serve.

Serves 2 (makes 10 pancakes)

SPROUTED BUCKWHEAT LOAF

INGREDIENTS

3 cups (495g/17.7oz) **buckwheat**, soaked (see page 11)
1 cup (160g/5.6oz) **flaxseeds**
1 cup (140g/4.9oz) **sunflower seeds**
3 Tbsp **rice malt syrup**
2 Tbsp **lemon juice**
½ cup (125ml) **coconut oil**
3 Tbsp **psyllium husk powder**
1 tsp **Himalayan sea salt**

METHOD

Strain the soaked buckwheat and rinse under clean, running water (until water runs clear). Place buckwheat in a food processor and add flaxseeds, sunflower seeds, rice malt syrup, lemon juice, coconut oil, psyllium husk powder and sea salt. Blend on low to gently mix all ingredients.

Using your hands, push the mixture into a 25.5 x 13.5 x 6cm loaf tin, pressing down firmly. Place gently upside down on a dehydrator tray that has been lined with baking paper. If you have pressed the bread down hard enough, it won't fall out of the tin.

Dehydrate for 12 hours. Over this time the bread will slowly release out of the tin and dehydrate on the outside edges. If after 8 hours the bread has not fallen out, gently tap the top to remove it from the tin.

After dehydrating, refrigerate the bread for 1 hour to cool down. Store, refrigerated, and eat within one week.

Makes one 25.5 x 13.5 x 6cm loaf

SEED LOAF FIVE WAYS

Each option covers two slices of Sprouted Buckwheat Loaf (see page 42).

RAWTELLA & STRAWBERRY

INGREDIENTS

3 cups (375g/13.2oz) **hazelnuts**
1 cup (200g/7oz) **coconut sugar**
½ cup (55g/2oz) **raw cacao powder**
1 tsp **Himalayan sea salt**
½ cup (125ml) **coconut oil**
4 **strawberries**
1 Tbsp **cacao nibs**, to garnish

METHOD

Place hazelnuts in a high-speed blender and blend on medium until smooth. Add coconut sugar, cacao powder and sea salt. Blend until well combined.

Pour into a bowl and, using your hands, massage in coconut oil. The rawtella should now be a smooth, spreadable consistency. Place three dollops on each piece of bread and spread evenly. Save extra rawtella in an airtight container in the pantry.

Hull the strawberries and slice lengthways. Place on top of the rawtella. Sprinkle with cacao nibs, if desired.

EDAMAME & PICKLED BEETROOT

INGREDIENTS

6 Tbsp **Edamame Guacamole**
(see page 124)
4 **Pickled Beetroots** (see page 240)
pinch of **freshly ground black
pepper**

METHOD

Spread the Edamame Guacamole on the bread. Finely slice the Pickled
Beetroot and arrange on top. Sprinkle with pepper.

BRUSCHETTA

INGREDIENTS

flesh of 1 **avocado**
juice of 2 **lemons**
pinch of **Himalayan sea salt**, plus
extra to serve
6 **cherry tomatoes**
3 Tbsp **extra virgin olive oil**
3 Tbsp **balsamic vinegar**
6 **basil leaves**
pinch of **freshly ground black
pepper**

METHOD

In a small bowl, mash avocado with lemon juice and sea salt. Spread the
mashed avocado on the bread. Halve the tomatoes and place on top of the
avocado. Drizzle with extra virgin olive oil and balsamic vinegar. Serve with
basil leaves and sprinkle with salt and pepper.

TAMARILLO, ALMOND & CINNAMON

INGREDIENTS

flesh of 2 tamarillos
2 Tbsp maple syrup
1 tsp cinnamon
10 almonds, chopped

METHOD

In a small bowl, mash tamarillo with a fork. Add maple syrup and cinnamon and mash again. Sieve to drain excess liquid. Spread mixture on the bread. Sprinkle almonds on top.

VANILLA MASCARPONE & BERRY CHIA JELLY

INGREDIENTS

6 Tbsp Vanilla Mascarpone (see page 38)
6 Tbsp Berry Chia Jelly (see page 39)
pinch of freeze-dried berries, to garnish

METHOD

Spread the Vanilla Mascarpone on the bread. Dollop the Berry Chia Jelly on top. Garnish with freeze-dried berries.

CHAI BANANA BREAD

INGREDIENTS

3 cups (375g/13.2oz) dehydrated almond pulp or 2½ cups (250g/8.8oz) almond flour

1 cup (160g/5.6oz) flaxseeds

½ tsp vanilla bean powder

1 tsp cinnamon

1 tsp ground clove

1 tsp freshly grated nutmeg

½ tsp freshly ground black pepper

1 tsp Himalayan sea salt

1 Tbsp ground ginger

4 bananas

½ cup (150g/5.3oz) maple syrup

⅓ cup (83ml) filtered water

1 cup (160g/5.6oz) dates, soaked for 4 hours

½ cup (65g/2.2oz) hazelnuts, chopped, plus extra to garnish

½ cup (50g/1.8oz) walnuts, chopped

METHOD

Line a 25.5 x 13.5 x 6cm loaf tin with baking paper. Place the almond pulp or flour, flaxseeds, vanilla bean powder, cinnamon, clove, nutmeg, pepper, sea salt and ginger in a blender and blend until fine. Add bananas, maple syrup, filtered water and dates and blend until smooth. Pour into a bowl and stir in hazelnuts and walnuts.

Press the mixture into the loaf tin and garnish with extra hazelnuts. Place in a dehydrator for 12 hours. Gently remove the loaf from the tin, peel back the baking paper from the edges, and leave in the dehydrator for another 12 hours.

Remove from dehydrator and refrigerate. Store in an airtight container and eat within seven days.

Makes one 25.5 x 13.5 x 6cm loaf

SALADS

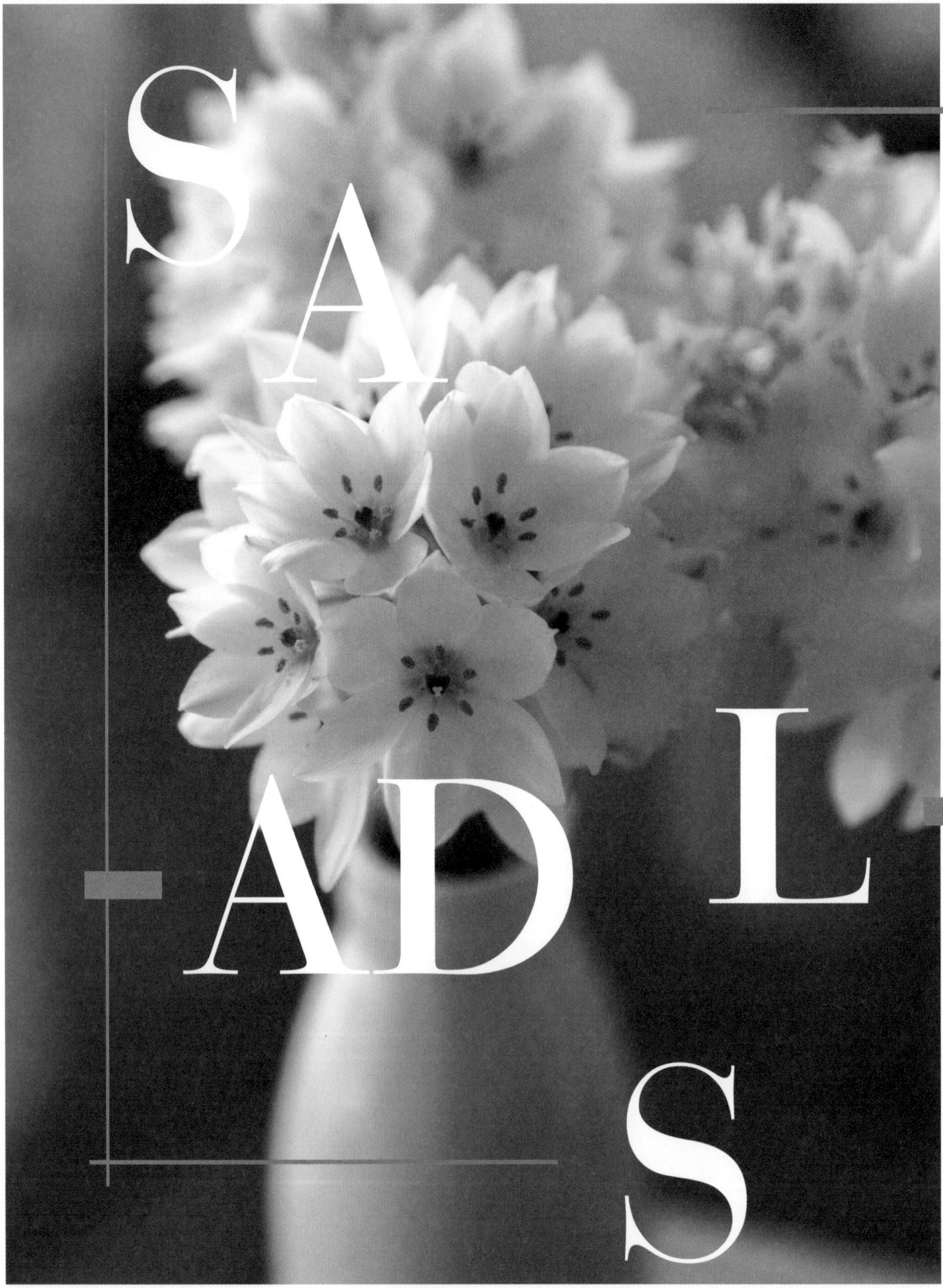

SALADS

BEETROOT RISOTTO WITH WASABI CREAM

INGREDIENTS

WASABI CREAM
1 cup (135g/4.8oz) **cashews**, soaked (see page 12)

½ cup (125ml) **filtered water**

1 tsp **wasabi powder**

1 Tbsp **rice malt syrup**

juice of 1 **lemon**

BEETROOT RISOTTO
4 **parsnips**

2 large **beetroots**

3 Tbsp finely chopped **chives**

1 clove **garlic**, minced

1 tsp **Himalayan sea salt**

1 tsp **freshly ground black pepper**

1 tsp **kelp powder**

1 Tbsp **miso paste**

5 Tbsp **sesame oil**

GARNISH
microherbs

METHOD

To make the wasabi cream, place all ingredients in a high-speed blender, and blend on high until smooth. Pour wasabi cream into a jug and set aside.

To make the risotto, peel the parsnips and beetroots, trim off the tops and bottoms and discard. Chop vegetables into pieces and place in a food processor. Process on medium until vegetables form a rice-like consistency, then place the 'risotto rice' into a bowl. Add the chives, garlic, sea salt, pepper, kelp powder, miso paste and sesame oil and mix thoroughly.

Place the risotto into short tumblers and press down firmly. Place your serving plate on top of the tumbler, and carefully flip so that the risotto falls onto the plate in a moulded form. Garnish with microherbs of your choice. Drizzle the wasabi cream around the outside of the risotto.

Serves 2

TIP

If you cannot source wasabi powder, use wasabi in a tube instead. It is best to add this to taste, as wasabi strength varies depending on the brand.

CARROT, LIME & COCONUT SALAD

INGREDIENTS

10 **carrots**, peeled and grated
½ cup (13g/0.5oz) **mint leaves**
½ cup (13g/0.5oz) **coriander leaves**
½ cup (50g/1.8oz) **dried coconut chips**, plus extra to garnish
½ cup (85g/3oz) **currants**

DRESSING
½ cup (125ml) **coconut aminos**
juice of 2 **limes**
¼ cup (65ml) **extra virgin olive oil**
juice and **rind** of 1 **orange**
½ cup (125ml) **coconut milk**
¼ cup (50g/1.8oz) **coconut sugar**
1 thumb **fresh ginger**
1 clove **garlic**
1 tsp **Himalayan sea salt**

METHOD

In a bowl, combine carrot with mint, coriander, coconut chips and currants and set aside.

To make the dressing, place all ingredients in a high-speed blender and blend until smooth. Pour the dressing over the salad and mix thoroughly. Serve in bowls and garnish with some extra coconut chip.

Serves 4

CORN & CUCUMBER CEVICHE

INGREDIENTS

¾ cup (150g/5.4oz) **corn**

1 yellow **capsicum**, diced

1 **telegraph cucumber**, diced

flesh of 1 **avocado**, chopped

4 Tbsp chopped **chives**

3 Tbsp diced **red onion**

2 Tbsp **basil leaves**

3 Tbsp **pine nuts**, plus extra to garnish

DRESSING

2 cloves **garlic**

juice of 1 **lemon**

1 Tbsp **nutritional yeast**

1 Tbsp **apple cider vinegar**

1 Tbsp **tahini**

1 tsp **Himalayan sea salt**

1 tsp **freshly ground black pepper**

METHOD

In a bowl, combine all the salad ingredients, mix thoroughly and set aside.

To make the dressing, place all ingredients in a high-speed blender and blend until smooth. Pour the dressing over the salad and mix thoroughly. Serve in bowls and garnish with pine nuts.

Serves 2 as a main, or 4 as a side salad

FATOUSH SALAD

INGREDIENTS

2 heads **cos lettuce**

4 **red radishes**

3 **tomatoes**, diced

1 **telegraph cucumber**, diced

½ cup (13g/0.5oz) **mint leaves**

½ cup (13g/0.5oz) roughly chopped **coriander leaves**

½ cup (13g/0.5oz) finely chopped **Italian parsley**

juice of 4 lemons

4 Tbsp **extra virgin olive oil**

1 Tbsp **sumac**

4 slices **Sprouted Buckwheat Loaf** (see page 42) or your preferred bread, diced

METHOD

Slice the lettuce leaves into strips and place in a bowl. Trim tops off the radishes and discard. Finely slice radishes using a sharp knife or mandolin. Slice in half again and add to bowl. Add tomato, cucumber, mint leaves, coriander leaves and parsley. Pour the lemon juice, olive oil and sumac over the top and mix thoroughly. Place salad in serving bowls and serve with diced bread cubes.

Serves 2 as main, 4 as a side salad

HEIRLOOM TOMATO CARPACCIO

INGREDIENTS

4 large **heirloom tomatoes**

10 **cherry tomatoes**

4 Tbsp **extra virgin olive oil**

2 tsp **Himalayan sea salt**

2 tsp **freshly ground black pepper**, plus extra to serve

flesh of 2 **avocados**

juice of 2 **lemons**

10 **basil leaves**, to serve

METHOD

Using a serrated knife or mandolin, cut heirloom tomatoes into thin slices. Arrange in bowls, layering colours. Slice cherry tomatoes and arrange on top. Drizze olive oil and 1 teaspoon each of salt and pepper over the tomatoes.

In a separate bowl, mash the avocado flesh with lemon juice and 1 teaspoon each of salt and pepper. When avocado is thoroughly mixed, dollop 2–3 tablespoons into the centre of each dish. Serve with basil leaves and extra pepper, to taste.

Serves 2 as a main, or 4 as a side

TIP

I adore this salad – it is so simple but full of flavour. This recipe belongs to my partner Joss, who I think makes this dish the best. It is so quick to whip up and makes for an delicious summer lunch or the perfect accompaniment to a dinner dish, especially raw pizza.

JAPANESE SLAW

INGREDIENTS

5 red radishes
1 red cabbage
1 savoy cabbage
500g/17.6oz mung bean sprouts
½ cup (13g/0.5oz) mint leaves
¾ cup (105g/3.6oz) raw peanuts
1 cup (200g/7oz) edamame beans
⅓ cup (50g/1.7oz) black sesame
seeds, plus extra to garnish

DRESSING
1 thumb fresh ginger
1 Tbsp chopped fresh chilli
juice of 4 lemons
3 Tbsp miso paste
¼ cup (63ml) apple cider vinegar
¼ cup (75g/2.6oz) rice malt syrup
½ cup (70g/2.4oz) cashews,
soaked (see page 12)
¼ cup (63ml) liquid aminos
(optional)
1 tsp Himalayan sea salt

METHOD

Trim the tops from the radishes and discard. Halve the radishes. Then using a sharp knife or mandolin, finely slice the radishes and place in a bowl. Slice cabbage leaves into fine strips and cut again into thirds. Add cabbage to the bowl with the mung bean sprouts, mint leaves, peanuts, edamame beans and black sesame seeds, and set aside.

To make the dressing, place all ingredients in a high-speed blender and blend on high until smooth. Pour the dressing into the bowl and mix thoroughly. Serve in bowls and garnish with extra sesame seeds.

Serves 4

MEX BOWL WITH COCONUT AVOCADO MOUSSE

INGREDIENTS

1 cauliflower
1 broccoli
1 red capsicum, finely chopped
12 cherry tomatoes, diced
¾ cup (150g/5.4oz) corn kernels
⅓ cup (50g/1.7oz) diced red onion
½ cup (13g/0.5oz) roughly
chopped coriander leaves
1 tsp Himalayan sea salt
1 tsp freshly ground black pepper

DRESSING
½ cup (125ml) apple cider vinegar
juice of 4 lemons

MOUSSE
flesh of 2 avocadoes
1 cup (250ml) coconut cream

GARNISH
1 tsp chopped fresh chilli

METHOD

Chop the cauliflower and broccoli roughly into small pieces and place in a food processor. Pulse so that the broccoli and cauliflower form a chunky rice-like consistency. Place in a bowl and add the rest of the ingredients. Pour apple cider vinegar and lemon juice over the salad, and mix thoroughly.

To make the mousse, place the avocado and coconut cream in a high-speed blender and blend until smooth.

Serve in the dressed salad bowls and place three large dollops of mousse on top of each. Garnish with a sprinkle of fresh chilli.

Serves 4

MOROCCAN BOWL

INGREDIENTS

1 cauliflower
6 carrots, peeled and grated
½ cup (85g/3oz) sultanas
½ cup (65g/2.3oz) roughly
chopped hazelnuts, plus extra
to garnish
½ cup (10g/0.4oz) finely
chopped curly parsley
¼ cup (40g/1.3oz) finely chopped
red onion
1 Tbsp turmeric

DRESSING
½ cup (120g/4.2oz) tahini
½ cup (125ml) lemon juice
¼ cup (63ml) extra virgin olive oil
3 cloves garlic
1 Tbsp coriander seeds
1 Tbsp caraway seeds
1 tsp cumin seeds
1 tsp chilli flakes

METHOD

Chop the cauliflower roughly into small pieces, discarding the stalk.
Place the cauliflower in a food processor and pulse until fine. Add carrot,
sultanas, hazelnuts, parsley, red onion and turmeric and mix thoroughly.

To make the dressing, place all ingredients in a high-speed blender and
blend until smooth. Pour the dressing over the salad and mix thoroughly.

Serve in bowls and garnish with extra chopped hazelnuts.

Serves 2 as a main, 4 as a side

NORTH AFRICAN SALAD

INGREDIENTS

2 eggplants

2 capsicums

1 cup (250ml) extra virgin olive oil

1 tsp Himalayan sea salt

1 tsp freshly ground black pepper

½ cup (13g/0.5oz) mint leaves

⅔ cup (18g/0.6oz) coriander leaves

½ red onion

juice of 3 lemons

seeds of 1 pomegranate

½ cup (65g/2.3oz) chopped pistachios

½ tsp ground cardamom

½ tsp ground cinnamon

1 tsp ground cumin

1 tsp ground coriander seeds

1 tsp ground caraway seeds

PRESERVED
LEMON DRESSING
(OPTIONAL)

2 Preserved Lemons
(see page 238)

½ cup (125ml) filtered water

⅓ cup (100g/3.5oz) rice malt syrup

METHOD

Trim tops and bottoms from eggplants and capsicums and discard. Dice eggplants and capsicums and place in a bowl. Add olive oil and a pinch of salt and pepper and mix with your hands, making sure the oil is absorbed by the vegetables. Place on a dehydrator tray and dehydrate for 2–3 hours. Place the dehydrated eggplant and capsicum into a mixing bowl and add the rest of the ingredients. Mix thoroughly and place salad in bowls.

To make the preserved lemon dressing, blend all dressing ingredients in a high-speed blender until smooth. Drizzle over the salad or serve in a jug.

Serves 2 as a main, 4 as a side

PAD THAI SALAD

INGREDIENTS

8 carrots

8 zucchinis

1 **shallot**, finely sliced

3 cups (450g/15.6oz) **mung bean sprouts**

2 **spring onions**, white removed and roughly sliced

½ cup (70g/2.4oz) **raw peanuts**, plus extra to garnish

½ cup (13g/0.5oz) roughly chopped **coriander leaves**, plus extra to garnish

1 **lemon**, quartered, to serve

DRESSING

3 **thumbs ginger**

½ cup (70g/2.4oz) raw peanuts

⅓ cup (83ml) **tamari**

juice of 4 lemons

⅓ cup (100g/3.5oz) **rice malt syrup**

¼ cup (63ml) **extra virgin olive oil**

⅓ cup (83ml) **coconut milk**

2 tsp **chilli flakes**

METHOD

Trim tops and bottoms from carrots and zucchinis and discard. Spiralise the carrots and zucchinis. If you are using a mandolin or sharp knife, create noodles by cutting the vegetables into thin strips, and slicing again into thin noodles. Place in a bowl and add shallot, mung bean sprouts, spring onion, peanuts and coriander leaves. Mix thoroughly and set aside.

To make the dressing, combine all dressing ingredients in a high-speed blender and blend until smooth. Pour over the salad and mix throughly.

Serve the salad in bowls with a wedge of lemon. Garnish with extra peanuts and coriander.

Serves 2 as a main, 4 as a side dish

TURKISH BOWL

INGREDIENTS

PICKLED CAULIFLOWER
225g/8oz cauliflower
2 cups (500ml) apple cider vinegar
3 tsp turmeric

TURKISH BOWL
1 iceberg lettuce
½ red onion, finely chopped
1 tomato, diced
1 cup (20g/0.7oz) parsley leaves
⅓ cup (83ml) extra virgin olive oil
juice of 4 lemons

TO SERVE
4 Tbsp Black Olive Tapenade
(see page 124)
6 Falafel (see page 85)
4 Tbsp Sauerkraut (see page 236)

GARNISH
1 Tbsp black sesame seeds

METHOD

Make the pickled cauliflower a day in advance. Chop the cauliflower into small pieces, keeping small florets intact, and immerse in a bowl of apple cider vinegar. Add turmeric and mix well. Cover and refrigerate to soak overnight.

To make the turkish bowl, finely slice the iceberg lettuce and place in a large bowl. Add red onion, tomato and parsley, and toss with olive oil and lemon juice. To serve, place salad in bowls and arrange the Black Olive Tapenade, Falafel, Sauerkraut and pickled cauliflower evenly on top. Garnish with black sesame seeds.

Serves 2

STRAWBERRY, WATERCRESS & ALMOND FETA SALAD

This is one of my favourite salads to take with me in a jar if I am on the go. I put the dressing in a small jar and the fresh ingredients in a big jar, then dress the salad when it gets to lunchtime.

INGREDIENTS

4 cups (80g/2.8oz) **watercress**

2 cups (300g/10.4oz) **mung bean sprouts**

5 large **strawberries**

flesh of 1 **avocado**, diced

½ **shallot**, finely sliced

10 **red cherry tomatoes**, halved

BALSAMIC DRESSING

¼ cup (63ml) **macadamia oil** or **extra virgin olive oil**

¼ cup (63ml) **coconut aminos** (optional)

3 Tbsp **balsamic vinegar**

TO SERVE

8 cloves **black garlic**

¾ cup (195g/6.9oz) **Almond Feta** (see page 132)

METHOD

Place watercress and mung bean sprouts in a mixing bowl. Hull the strawberries, slice and add to the bowl. Add avocado, shallot and cherry tomatoes.

To make the balsamic dressing, place all dressing ingredients in a jar, secure the lid tightly and shake until well mixed.

Pour dressing over salad and mix thoroughly. Arrange on plates. To serve, place black garlic cloves evenly on each plate and add 3–4 dollops of Almond Feta.

Serves 2 as a main, 4 as a side salad

TIP

Note that black garlic is not raw, but I occasionally use it in recipes to bring a new element of flavour and texture. Black garlic has a savoury sweet flavour similar to a combination of balsamic vinegar and roasted garlic. It also has many health benefits. To keep this recipe completely raw, omit it.

TABOULI

INGREDIENTS

1 cauliflower
1 **telegraph cucumber**, diced
12 **cherry tomatoes**, halved
1 cup (20g/0.7oz) finely chopped **curly parsley**
2 **spring onions**, chopped
3 Tbsp **black sesame seeds**, plus extra to garnish

DRESSING
½ cup (120g/4.2oz) **tahini**
⅓ cup (83ml) **lemon juice**
1 tsp **salt**
1 tsp **freshly ground black pepper**
1 clove **garlic**
⅓ cup (83ml) **filtered water**

METHOD

Chop the cauliflower into small pieces, removing the stalk. Place in a food processor and blend until cauliflower resembles crumbs. Place in a bowl and add cucumber, tomatoes, parsley, spring onions and black sesame seeds.

To make the dressing, place all ingredients in a high-speed blender, and blend until smooth.

Pour dressing over salad and mix thoroughly. Serve in bowls and garnish with a pinch of black sesame seeds.

Serves 2 as a main, 4 as a side dish

MEDITATION

Namaste: The light in me honours the light in you.

After practising meditation for five years I can truly say it has changed my view of myself, others and life. Meditation has become very important to me and without it I feel quite strung out. I feel naturally more connected to people and myself after meditation; I feel happier and life feels easier.

It took me a few weeks to really start to see the difference in my daily life. I almost gave up, not thinking that I could notice any immediate benefits. However, after sticking to a routine for five minutes a day, my life became very different.

It took real commitment, but change became so profound, I felt like a brand-new person. My relationships improved, I had more energy, my life fell into place, I had greater trust in my gut instinct and I found a natural confidence that came with ease.

Meditation has also helped me find happiness in the moment: the feeling of not wanting or needing anything, but being simply content with what is. Every now and then during the day, I will stop briefly and pause for a moment and feel truly content. I know this is because of my meditation practice.

Meditation is a way of resetting your mind to a place where it is just you, in your space, making peace with yourself. Meditation has been around for thousands of years, originally being a religious practise, but over time has become a scientifically recognised form of physiological and psychological healing.

Meditation is a way of becoming aware of your thoughts and calming your mind. We are used to having an overflow of thoughts such as what we need to remember for work tomorrow, what to have for breakfast, or organising the kids' birthday parties. Calming the mind is a way of filtering out the noise and resetting the brain in a quiet space.

Between 10 and 20 minutes is as little as it takes to feel refreshed, energised and at peace.

Research has found that people who meditate see their doctors less, have a lessened dependence on alcohol and cigarettes and also have decreased depression, anxiety and irritability.

Once you see how powerful meditation is, you won't want to stop. It can lead to many other different types of spiritual experiences and awakenings, through practice and experimentation.

HOW TO MEDITATE

1. Set your timer between 10 and 20 minutes.

2. Sit in your favourite room.

3. Light your favourite candle or incense.

4. Make sure your space is quiet, warm and comfortable.

5. Sit on your favourite chair, placing your hands in your lap. You may also lie down, or sit in a lotus position with your hands resting on your knees.

6. Close your eyes and turn your attention inwards.

7. Imagine a stream of light energy filling your body from the infinite source above. Imagine it filling your body from the top of your head, right down through your neck, chest and stomach, and down to the tips of your toes.

8. Continue to feel the light energy streaming down through your head and filtering through your body. Enjoy the feeling of lightness and subtle energy.

9. Focus on stillness, focus on your inner light, focus on bringing in love.

10. When you are ready to finish your meditation, bring your hands in to prayer position, and whisper "namaste".

A HEALTHY LIFE

While I advocate a healthy life, it is just as important to maintain balance. I don't believe in diets, fads or trends that focus on cutting out certain 'bad foods' or weight loss. Living well and being happy in our bodies is about nourishment, abundance and balance. Being healthy is listening to what makes us feel good, eating plenty of fresh fruits and vegetables and focusing on not just physical wellness, but mental and emotional wellness too.

A SUSTAINABLE DIET

Any diet can help you lose weight, if that is your target goal. However, the real goal to me is health, feeling good about yourself and feeling confident about your body.

If you focus on calories, consumption, weight and measurements, you will have a mindset which will ultimately lead to imbalance. Imbalance can bring about an unhealthy relationship with food.

This is what scares me about people following diets: it leads to an unhealthy way of viewing food and yourself; it creates low self-esteem. It is my goal to help people realise that they don't need to think like this in order to live a healthy, fulfilled life. Your relationship with food must be the same as your relationship with yourself: kind, nourishing and loving.

Balance to me is about keeping an open mind. When people ask me if I'm a raw vegan, I answer with, "I don't label myself with anything." The healthiest approach to eating well is to have the mentality that you are eating healthy foods because that is what you want to eat. I crave fresh foods over fried foods, so that is why I eat them. If my body asks me for fresh fruit in the morning, then I give it fresh fruit; if it asks me for something hot, then I give something hot. And, honestly, if my body asks me for something non-vegan, then I give it that too (it doesn't happen very often). It is so important to do what's right for you.

Occasionally, when my partner cooks us dinner or I go to my mum's house for dinner, then I eat meat too! I never restrict myself, and while I know that ideally I would love to eat 80 percent raw food, sometimes life just gets in the way and it isn't possible.

BALANCE

There are things that are purely just good for the soul, and let us feel that we are eating in a way that is sustainable long term. If we told ourselves we were only allowed 100 percent vegan or uncooked food, having a glass of wine in the evenings would be off-limits.

The thing about this is that letting ourselves live a little is good for our souls! It is so important to maintain balance, and remember to have fun too.

I often turn down invitations to big drinking occasions as I no longer find alcohol serves me well, but I will almost always take up an invitation to have a glass of wine with a good friend.

Finding what works for you is the best way of finding balance.

LUNCH

ONION WRAP

INGREDIENTS

WRAP
3 large **red onions**
¾ cup (120g/4.2oz) **flaxmeal**
¾ cup (105g/3.9oz) **sunflower seeds**
¼ cup (63ml) **tamari**
⅓ cup (83ml) **olive oil**
3 Tbsp **maple syrup**
½ tsp **Himalayan sea salt**
½ tsp **freshly ground black pepper**

FILLING
1 cup (150g/5.2oz) **mung bean sprouts**
1 cup (150g/5.2oz) grated **carrot**
½ cup (50g/1.8oz) shredded **red cabbage**
flesh of ½ **avocado**
½ cup (75g/2.6oz) **Black Olive Tapenade** (see page 124)
3 Tbsp **Aioli** (see page 235)

GARNISH
coriander leaves

METHOD

To make the wrap, peel and finely slice onions, then place in food processor. Add the rest of the wrap ingredients and process on low for 2 minutes, scraping the sides of the bowl down occasionally with a spatula. Spread mixture, about 2mm deep, onto two lined dehydrator trays. Dehydrate for 3 hours. Flip onto the other side and return to the dehydrator for another 3 hours.

Use immediately or store in an airtight container for up to 3 days. Do not refrigerate as it will go hard.

To make the filling, arrange sprouts, carrot, cabbage and avocado in the centre of the wraps. Spread filling to the edges of the wraps. Place the Black Olive Tapenade on top, and drizzle with Aioli. Wrap the onion wrap around, sushi-style, and cut in half. Sometimes I use a piece of string to tie around the wrap to hold in place. Garnish with coriander.

Serves 2

EGGPLANT BACON

INGREDIENTS

¼ cup (75g/2.6oz) **maple syrup**

⅓ cup (83ml) **tamari**

⅓ tsp **liquid smoke** (optional)

¼ cup (63ml) **apple cider vinegar**

¼ cup (63ml) **olive oil**

1 tsp **smoked paprika**

½ tsp **ground cumin**

1 **eggplant**

METHOD

Place maple syrup, tamari, liquid smoke, apple cider vinegar, olive oil, smoked paprika and cumin in a high-speed blender and blend until smooth. Set aside.

Slice the top and bottom off the eggplant. Using a mandolin, slice the eggplant lengthways (slices should be about 2mm in width). Place each slice in a shallow dish, layering the eggplant until you have used up all the slices. Pour the blended mixture over the eggplant, making sure the entire top surface is covered. Leave to marinate for 1 hour.

Place the eggplant slices on dehydrator trays, making sure not to overlap the pieces as this slows down drying time. Dehydrate for 12 hours, or until preferred texture is reached. Store, refrigerated, in an airtight container for up to one week.

Makes 50 slices

FALAFEL

INGREDIENTS

1½ cups (210g/7.4oz) **sunflower seeds**

1 cup (160g/5.6oz) **flaxseeds**

3 Tbsp **tamari**

2 cups (40g/1.4oz) **parsley**

juice of 4 **lemons**

3 cloves **garlic**

½ cup (75g/2.6oz) **white sesame seeds**

METHOD

Blend sunflower seeds and flaxseeds in a food processor until fine. Add tamari, parsley, lemon juice and garlic. Pulse until the mixture becomes sticky.

Roll heaped tablespoonfuls of mixture into falafel shapes, then roll in white sesame seeds. Make sure falafel are completely coated in sesame seeds, then place onto a lined dehydrator tray. Dehydrate for 4 hours or until desired crunchiness is reached. Store in an airtight container for up to one week.

Makes 12

COLLARD WRAPS

INGREDIENTS

4 large, flat **collard green leaves**
5 Tbsp **Tabouli** (see page 76)
4 **Falafel** (see page 85)
3 Tbsp **alfalfa sprouts**
6 Tbsp **Aioli** (see page 235)

METHOD

Take 4 collard green leaves, placing the largest one in the centre of the chopping board in front of you with the stem closest to you and the dark side of the leaf facing down. Take 2 medium-sized leaves and place them on the left and right of the large leaf, slightly overlapping. Arrange so that the stems are touching in the centre. Place 5 heaped tablespoons of Tabouli in the centre of the leaves. Spread it two thirds of the way down and up to the top of the leaf. Place 3 Falafel along the centre on top of the Tabouli, followed by alfalfa sprouts.

Dress with the Aioli and place a small leaf on top, dark side facing out. Wrap up by folding the bottom up first, then the right side over, tucking the leaves underneath, and folding the left side over last.

Use a strip of baking paper to wrap around and hold in place, and use a piece of string to keep it tight. Enjoy immediately, or refrigerate in an airtight container for up to 48 hours.

Serves 1

TIP

If you can't source collard greens, large spinach leaves or iceberg lettuce leaves can also be used.

CREAMY CORN, COCONUT & HAZELNUT SOUP

INGREDIENTS

2 cups (500ml) coconut milk

1 cup (250ml) filtered water

2 cups (400g/14oz) fresh corn kernels

⅓ cup (40g/1.5oz) hazelnuts, plus extra to serve

1 tsp dried turmeric

1 Tbsp salt

1 tsp freshly ground black pepper

¼ cup sprigs of fresh dill, to serve

METHOD

Place all ingredients except dill in a high-speed blender and blend on medium for 2 minutes. Taste and add salt and pepper to your preference. To warm the soup, turn the blender to high and blend for 4–5 minutes. Pour into bowls and serve with some fresh dill and chopped hazelnuts on top.

Serves 4

CARROT, CUMIN & CORIANDER SOUP

INGREDIENTS

8 carrots, chopped
3 cups (750ml) coconut milk
3 tomatoes
1½ Tbsp ground cumin
2 Tbsp coriander seeds
3 Tbsp miso paste
1 tsp salt
2 tsp freshly ground black pepper
2 Tbsp yoghurt, to serve
¾ cup (21g/0.9oz) coriander leaves, plus extra to garnish

METHOD

Peel carrots and trim off the tops and bottoms. Chop into 2cm pieces and place in the high-speed blender. Add the rest of the ingredients to the blender. Blend on medium for 1–2 minutes or until preferred consistency is reached. Serve in bowls with a dollop of yoghurt and a sprig of coriander on top.

Serves 4

CUCUMBER GAZPACHO

INGREDIENTS

2 **telegraph cucumbers**
2 cloves **garlic**
½ cup (125ml) **lemon juice**
½ cup (13g/0.5oz) **coriander**
1 tsp **Himalayan sea salt**
1 tsp **freshly ground black pepper**
2 cups (500ml) **coconut milk**
1 Tbsp **apple cider vinegar**
1 Tbsp **chilli flakes** or chopped
fresh chilli, to garnish

METHOD

Roughly chop the cucumbers into pieces and place, with all the ingredients except the chilli, in a food processor and process on slow until smooth. Be careful not to process on a high speed, as air gets into the soup and creates foam.

Chill or serve immediately. Serve in small bowls and garnish with chilli flakes or fresh chilli.

Serves 2–4

NAKED REUBEN

This is my healthy take on the traditional 'Reuben', which is usually a toasted rye bread sandwich filled with Swiss cheese, corned beef, sauerkraut and Thousand Island dressing, and is popular in the USA.

INGREDIENTS

QUICK CHEESE
(MAKES 2½ CUPS)
2 cups (270g/9.6oz) cashews

juice of 1 lemon

2 Tbsp apple cider vinegar

1 Tbsp savoury yeast flakes

½ tsp Himalayan pink salt

½ tsp freshly ground black pepper

1 Tbsp agave nectar

⅓ cup (83ml) filtered water

2 Tbsp extra virgin olive oil

NAKED REUBEN
4 slices of Sprouted Buckwheat Loaf (see page 42) or your bread of preference

4 Tbsp Mustard (see page 238)

4 pieces Eggplant Bacon (see page 84)

4 Tbsp Sauerkraut (see page 236)

2 Tbsp microherbs or watercress

2 Tbsp Quick Cheese

METHOD

To make the quick cheese, place all ingredients in a high-speed blender, and blend until smooth. Scrape down the sides of the jug occasionally to ensure all ingredients are blended. Store in an airtight container in the refrigerator for up to two weeks.

To make the Naked Reuben, spread the Mustard on 2 slices of bread. Place 2 pieces of Eggplant Bacon on top of each one, followed by 2 tablespoons of Sauerkraut. Garnish with microherbs or watercress. Dollop a tablespoon of quick cheese on top of each, then place the remaining slices of bread on top.

Makes 2

RADICCHIO TACOS

INGREDIENTS

GUACAMOLE
flesh of 1 avocado
3 Tbsp lemon juice
½ tsp Himalayan sea salt
½ tsp freshly ground black pepper
2 Tbsp tamari (optional)

PINEAPPLE SALSA
10 cherry tomatoes, diced
½ cup (115g/4oz) finely chopped pineapple
juice of 4 lemons
¼ cup (7g/0.3oz) mint leaves
½ tsp Himalayan sea salt
½ chilli, seeds removed and finely sliced
½ cup (100g/3.5oz) corn kernels
¼ cup (7g/0.3oz) finely chopped coriander leaves, plus extra to garnish

TO SERVE
900g/32oz radicchio
2 cups (400g/14oz) Walnut Mince (see page 101)

METHOD

To make the guacamole, place avocado in a small bowl and mash with a fork. Add lemon juice, sea salt, pepper and tamari. Continue to mash until well combined and creamy. Set aside.

To make the salsa, combine cherry tomatoes, pineapple, lemon juice, mint, sea salt, chilli, corn and coriander leaves in a bowl. Stir until well mixed. Set aside.

Remove the stalk from radicchio and wash the leaves. Arrange leaves on two large plates. Place spoonfuls of Walnut Mince in each leaf, dollop guacamole on top, and dress with a spoonful of salsa. Garnish with a few extra coriander leaves.

Serves 2

TIP

You may like to lay all the components out on the table so that guests can help themselves, or arrange the made-up tacos on a plate.

DINNER

DINNER

CORN CHIPS

INGREDIENTS

1 cup (160g/5.6oz) **flaxseeds**
1 cup (250ml) **filtered water**
3 Tbsp **olive oil**
1 **shallot**
2 Tbsp **maple syrup**
1 clove **garlic**
1½ tsp **salt**
2½ tsp **turmeric**
2 Tbsp **nutritional yeast** (optional)
4 cups (800g/28oz) **corn kernels**

METHOD

Place all ingredients (corn last) in a high-speed blender and blend on medium for 2 minutes or until smooth, stirring occasionally. Pour the mixture across three dehydrator trays and, using a pallet knife, flatten so the mixture is 3mm deep. Dehydrate for 3 hours.

Using a pizza cutter or large knife, cut into triangles and place back in the dehydrator for a further 5 hours, or until your preferred crunchiness is reached. Store covered in the refrigerator for up to one week.

Makes 3 trays

WALNUT MINCE

INGREDIENTS

2 cups (200g/7oz) walnuts
1 Tbsp rice malt syrup
1 tsp smoked paprika
1 clove garlic
½ tsp ground cumin
½ tsp ground coriander
3 Tbsp tamari
1 tsp liquid smoke (optional)

METHOD

Place all ingredients in a food processor and process on medium for 2 minutes. Store, refrigerated, in an airtight container for up to two weeks.

Makes 2½ cups

LASAGNE

INGREDIENTS

10 zucchinis

1 broccoli head

½ cup (75g/2.6oz) sundried tomatoes

1 tsp Himalayan sea salt

1 cup (250g/8.8oz) Quick Cheese (see page 94)

1 cup (200g/7oz) Walnut Mince (see page 101)

½ cup (100g/3.5oz) Tomato Sauce (see page 234)

¼ cup (63ml) extra virgin olive oil

½ tsp freshly ground black pepper

⅓ cup (7g/0.3oz) fresh basil leaves, to garnish

METHOD

Trim the tops and bottoms from the zucchinis. Using a mandolin or a sharp knife, cut zucchinis into thin slices and set aside.

Process broccoli florets in a food processor until fine. Add sundried tomatoes and sea salt and process until well combined.

Arrange zucchini slices, lengthways, on a serving plate, making a square shape. I like to overlap the slices to ensure coverage of each layer. Spread the broccoli mixture on top and press with the back of a spoon to ensure the mixture is flat and packed down.

Place another layer of zucchini strips on top of the broccoli mixture. Spread the Quick Cheese over the zucchini, making sure it is spread evenly across the lasagne and reaches right to the edges.

Place another layer of zucchini strips on top of the Quick Cheese. Spread the Walnut Mince over the zucchini, again making sure it is spread evenly.

Place another layer of zucchini strips on top of the Walnut Mince. Spread the Tomato Sauce over the zucchini, again making sure it is spread evenly. Place the final layer of zucchini strips on top of the Tomato Sauce.

Drizzle with extra virgin olive oil, sprinkle with pepper and place basil leaves on top to garnish.

Serves 4–6

BURGERS

INGREDIENTS

BUNS
1 cup (90g/3.2oz) **gluten-free oats**
1½ cups (190g/6.6oz) **dehydrated almond pulp** or **almond flour**
⅓ cup (55g/1.9oz) **flaxseeds**
3 Tbsp **filtered water**
4 tsp **lemon juice**
3 Tbsp **rice malt syrup**
1 tsp **Himalayan sea salt**
pinch of **Himalayan pink salt**

FILLING
1 cup (200g/7oz) **Walnut Mince**
(see page 101)
⅓ cup (65g/2.3oz) **Tomato Sauce**
(see page 234)
4 leaves **iceberg lettuce**
1 Tbsp **Quick Cheese**
(see page 94)
1 **tomato**, sliced
2 **pickles**, sliced
½ **red onion**, sliced

METHOD

To make the buns, blend the oats in a high-speed blender until fine. Place in a bowl and set aside. Blend the almond pulp or flour until fine, and add to the oats. Add the rest of the ingredients and mix, using your hands, to form a dough. Add more water if needed. Divide the dough into four and mould each piece into a bun shape. Place in a dehydrator tray and dehydrate for 6 hours.

Use your hands to mould the Walnut Mince into a patty shape and set aside. Carefully cut each burger bun in half and lay open. Spread Tomato Sauce evenly onto each bottom half. Top with a lettuce leaf, 'mince' patty, a slice of cheese and slices of tomato, followed by pickles and red onion. Place other bun half on top.

Makes 4

CARROT FETTUCCINE

INGREDIENTS

8 **carrots**, peeled

½ cup (100g/3.5oz) **edamame beans**

1½ cups (490g/17.3oz) **Mushroom Sauce** (see page 114)

1 tsp **dried oregano**, plus extra to garnish

METHOD

Using a vegetable peeler, peel carrots into thin strips. Do this by holding the top of the carrot and starting to peel about 2cm from the top, sliding the peeler down to the bottom. At the end you will be left with a knob of carrot in your hand. You may use a mandolin for this; however, it must be on a very fine setting.

Place the carrot strips in a bowl and add edamame beans, Mushroom Sauce and oregano. Mix thoroughly until the carrot is well covered. Serve in bowls and garnish with extra oregano.

Serves 2

SPAGHETTI BOLOGNAISE

INGREDIENTS

MEATBALLS

2 cups (400g/14oz) Walnut Mince
(see page 101)

ZUCCHINI SPAGHETTI

10 large zucchinis

10 cherry tomatoes

⅓ cup (60g/2.1oz) black olives,
halved

BOLOGNAISE SAUCE

2 cup (300g/10.4oz) sundried or
dehydrated tomatoes

1 Tbsp chopped oregano leaves,
plus extra to garnish

1 Tbsp chopped rosemary leaves

½ cup (125ml) olive oil

METHOD

To make the meatballs, roll Walnut Mince into small balls. Place on a
dehydrator tray. Dehydrate for 6 hours or until your preferred crunchiness
is reached.

Once the meatballs are ready, make the spaghetti. If you have a spiraliser
or mandolin, use the tool to create zucchini spaghetti. If you don't have
either of these tools, use a sharp knife to trim the top and bottom from
the zucchinis. Thinly slice the zucchinis into strips, and then into long
spaghetti-like pieces. Place the zucchinis in a bowl and add olives
and tomatoes.

To make the bolognaise sauce, place all sauce ingredients in a food
processor and blend on medium until smooth. Add to the zucchini
spaghetti and mix well.

Divide the spaghetti evenly between bowls and top with meatballs.
Garnish with extra oregano.

Serves 2–4

PIZZA

INGREDIENTS

BASE
1 cup (90g/3.2oz) gluten-free oats

1½ cups (190g/6.6oz) dehydrated almond pulp or almond flour

⅓ cup (55g/1.9oz) flaxseeds

5 Tbsp filtered water

4 Tbsp lemon juice

3 Tbsp rice malt syrup

1 tsp Himalayan sea salt

¼ cup (60g/2.1oz) Irish Moss Paste (optional, see page 36)

TOPPING
½ cup (165g/5.8oz) Mango & Ginger Chutney (see page 235)

½ red onion, thinly sliced

⅓ cup (9g/0.3oz) coriander leaves

10 Tbsp Almond Feta (see page 132)

⅓ cup (55g/1.9oz) diced fresh pineapple

¼ cup (35g/1.2oz) cashews

METHOD

To make the pizza base, place oats in a high-speed blender and blend on high until fine. Place oats in a bowl and add the rest of the base ingredients. Using your hands, massage the mixture until a dough forms. Add a splash of water if it's too crumbly. Roll the dough into a ball and place on a square of baking paper. Place another piece of baking paper on top and, using a rolling pin, roll the dough out into a circle. You may need to use a knife to trim dough into a circle. Place in a dehydrator for 4–6 hours.

To make the topping, spread Mango & Ginger Chutney to the edges of the pizza base. Arrange onion and coriander leaves on top. Cut pizza in half, then quarters, then each quarter in half, so you end up with eight slices. Place dollops of Almond Feta on cut pizza, then finish by scattering pineapple and cashews on top.

Serves 8

MACADAMIA CHEESE & CARAMELISED ONION TARTS

INGREDIENTS

TART CASES
2 cups (180g/6.4oz) gluten-free oats
2 cups (270g/9.6oz) cashews
½ shallot, peeled and chopped
3 Tbsp filtered water
3 Tbsp extra virgin olive oil
½ tsp salt
½ tsp freshly ground black pepper

CARAMELISED ONION
½ red onion
1 Tbsp extra virgin olive oil
3 Tbsp coconut sugar

SEMI-DRIED TOMATOES
10 cherry tomatoes, halved
1 Tbsp extra virgin olive oil

MACADAMIA CHEESE
2 cups (270g/9.6oz) macadamias
1 cup (250ml) filtered water
2 Tbsp extra virgin olive oil
2 Tbsp nutritional yeast
1 tsp salt
1 tsp freshly ground black pepper
juice of 2 lemons
2 cloves garlic

GARNISH
4 Tbsp balsamic vinegar
pinch salt
pinch freshly ground black pepper
8 basil leaves

METHOD

To make the tart cases, place oats in a high-speed blender and blend until fine. Transfer to a bowl. Place cashews in the blender and blend until fine. Add to the oats. Place shallot, filtered water, and extra virgin olive oil in the blender and blend until smooth. Add to the blended oats and cashews. Add salt and pepper and, using your hands, massage until a dough forms. Divide the dough into four pieces and press each piece into a 6–8cm tart tin. Place tins in dehydrator and dehydrate for 12 hours.

To make the caramelised onion, slice red onion into strips. Place in a small bowl and rub with olive oil and coconut sugar. Place on a dehydrator tray and dehydrate for 3 hours.

To make the semi-dried tomatoes, place halved cherry tomatoes on a dehydrator tray, face up, and drizzle with olive oil. Dehydrate for 3 hours.

To make the macadamia cheese, place all ingredients in a high-speed blender and blend on medium until smooth.

Carefully remove the tart cases from the tins. Pour the macadamia cheese evenly into each of the tart cases. Decorate one side of the tarts with caramelised onion and the other side with semi-dried tomatoes. Sprinkle each tart with a tablespoon of balsamic vinegar and a pinch of salt and pepper and garnish with two basil leaves.

Serve immediately or store in an airtight container for up to three days.

Makes 4 tarts

MUSHROOM & ASPARAGUS TARTS

INGREDIENTS

TART CASES
2 cups (180g/6.4oz) **gluten-free oats**

2 cups (270g/9.6oz) **cashews**

½ **shallot**, peeled and chopped

3 Tbsp **filtered water**

3 Tbsp **extra virgin olive oil**

½ tsp **salt**

½ tsp **freshly ground black pepper**

DEHYDRATED VEGETABLES
2½ cups (375g/13.2oz) peeled and sliced **mushrooms** (makes 2 cups dehydrated mushrooms)

10 spears **asparagus**

3 Tbsp **extra virgin olive oil**

pinch of **Himalayan sea salt**

MUSHROOM SAUCE (MAKES 3 CUPS)
2 cups (270g/9.6oz) **cashews**

1 clove **garlic**

½ **shallot**

¼ cup (63ml) **extra virgin olive oil**

1 tsp **Himalayan sea salt**

½ tsp **freshly ground black pepper**

2 tsp **apple cider vinegar**

1 tsp **dulse flakes**

1½ cup (115g/3.9oz) **dehydrated mushrooms**(see above)

¾ cup (190ml) **filtered water**

TO SERVE
10 spears **dehydrated asparagus** (see previous column)

½ cup (40g/1.3oz) **dehydrated mushrooms**(see previous column)

1 Tbsp **truffle oil**

pinch of **freshly ground black pepper**

3 Tbsp chopped **fresh chives**

METHOD

To make the tart cases, place oats in a high-speed blender and blend until fine. Transfer to a bowl. Place cashews in the blender and blend until fine. Add to the oats. Place shallot, filtered water, and extra virgin olive oil in the blender and blend until smooth. Add to the blended oats and cashews. Add salt and pepper and, using your hands, massage until a dough forms. Divide the dough into four pieces and press each piece into a 6–8cm tart tin. Place tins in dehydrator and dehydrate for 12 hours.

To make the dehydrated vegetables, place mushrooms and asparagus on a dehydrator tray. Drizzle with olive oil and sea salt, and dehydrate for 45 minutes.

To make the mushroom sauce, place all ingredients in a high-speed blender and blend on medium until smooth. Pour evenly into each tart case.

Chop dehydrated asparagus spears into 5cm pieces and serve with the tarts along with the remaining dehydrated mushrooms. Sprinkle each tart with truffle oil, pepper and chives.

Makes 4 tarts

NACHOS

INGREDIENTS

1 batch of **Corn Chips**
(see page 100)
1 batch of **Walnut Mince**
(see page 101)

GUACAMOLE
flesh of 2 **avocados**
juice of 2 **limes**
1 Tbsp finely diced **fresh chilli**
1 tsp **Himalayan sea salt**
1 tsp **freshly ground black pepper**

SALSA
3 **tomatoes**, finely diced
½ **red capsicum**, diced
⅓ cup (7g/0.3oz) **coriander leaves**
juice of 3 **lemons**
⅓ cup (65g/2.3oz) **corn kernels**
¼ cup (40g/1.3oz) diced **red onion**
1 tsp **Himalayan sea salt**

CHIMICHURRI
1 cup (20g/0.7oz) **parsley leaves**
⅓ cup (9g/0.3oz) **coriander leaves**
2 Tbsp **oregano leaves**
2 cloves **garlic**
½ cup (125ml) **extra virgin olive oil**
juice of 4 **lemons**
1 tsp **Himalayan sea salt**
½ tsp **freshly ground black pepper**

METHOD

To make the guacamole, mash avocado flesh until creamy. Add the rest of the ingredients and mix well.

To make the salsa, place all ingredients in a small bowl and mix well.

To make the chimichurri, place all ingredients in a food processor and blend until smooth. Pour into a jar and store in the fridge.

Arrange corn chips on serving plates. Place Walnut Mince on top. Dollop guacamole and salsa on top of the corn chips. Dress with chimichurri.

Serves 4

MASSAMAN CURRY
WITH COCONUT CAULIFLOWER RICE

INGREDIENTS

MAPLE VEGETABLES
1 zucchini

1 bok choy

1 large carrot

¼ red cabbage

3 Tbsp miso paste

3 Tbsp maple syrup

COCONUT CAULIFLOWER RICE
1 cauliflower

3 Tbsp coconut oil

⅓ cup (35g/1.2oz) desiccated coconut

3 Tbsp black sesame seeds

1 tsp salt

MASSAMAN CURRY
4 cups (1L) coconut milk

4 Tbsp miso paste

2 Tbsp coconut sugar

¼ cup raw peanuts

1 clove garlic

½ shallot

½ cup coriander leaves

1 tsp Himalayan sea salt

1 tsp grated fresh ginger

SPICE MIX
1 tsp turmeric

½ tsp ground cinnamon

1 tsp coriander seeds

¼ tsp cardamom seeds

½ tsp whole cloves

½ tsp ground nutmeg

1½ tsp ground cumin

½ tsp chilli flakes

METHOD

To make the maple vegetables, slice zucchini, bok choy, carrot and red cabbage into bite-sized pieces. Place the vegetables in a bowl and combine with the miso paste and maple syrup. Mix until the vegetables are well covered in the marinade. Place on a dehydrator tray and dehydrate for 1–2 hours.

To make the coconut cauliflower rice, chop cauliflower florets into chunks and place in a food processor. Add the rest of the ingredients and pulse until a rice-like consistency forms. Set aside.

To make the massaman curry, place all curry ingredients in a high-speed blender and blend until smooth. Place all spice mix ingredients in a mortar and pestle and grind until fine. Add to the curry mixture in the blender and blend further until well combined. Pour the curry into serving bowls and arrange maple vegetables evenly on top. Serve with coconut cauliflower rice.

Serves 2

RAMEN

INGREDIENTS

3 zucchinis
4 cups (1L) filtered water
1 tsp grated fresh ginger
1 clove garlic
3 Tbsp sesame oil
4 Tbsp tamari
2 Tbsp ponzu (optional)
1 tsp Himalayan sea salt
1 tsp freshly ground black pepper
2 Tbsp wakame fronds
1 cup mung bean sprouts
6 Tbsp finely sliced spring onion
6 shiitake mushrooms, sliced
⅓ cup (45g/1.6oz) crushed raw
peanuts
2 tsp black sesame seeds,
to garnish

METHOD

If you have a spiraliser or mandolin, use the tool to create zucchini noodles. If you don't have either of these tools, use a sharp knife to trim the top and bottom from the zucchinis. Thinly slice the zucchinis into strips, and then into long noodle-like pieces. Place the zucchini in a bowl and set aside.

Place 4 cups of hot water in a high-speed blender with the ginger, garlic, sesame oil, tamari, ponzu, sea salt and pepper. Blend on medium to combine all ingredients, then blend for 3–4 minutes more to warm the liquid.

Pour broth into serving bowls and place a tablespoon of wakame fronds in each bowl. Stir slightly so the fronds begin to absorb liquid. Add the zucchini noodles to each bowl. Arrange equal amounts of sprouts, spring onion, mushrooms and peanuts on top, then garnish with black sesame seeds.

Serves 2

ENTERTAINING

ENTERTAINING

BLACK OLIVE TAPENADE

INGREDIENTS

1 cup (100g/3.5oz) walnuts
1 cup (180g/6.3oz) pitted black olives
1 tsp salt
½ cup (125ml) extra virgin olive oil

METHOD

Place all ingredients in the food processor bowl and process on medium until well combined. I prefer my tapenade a bit chunky; however, if you prefer a smoother consistency, blend for longer. Transfer to a bowl and serve. Store in an airtight container in the refrigerator for up to one week.

Makes 2 cups

EDAMAME GUACAMOLE

INGREDIENTS

3 cups (600g/21oz) edamame beans
2 Tbsp extra virgin olive oil
1 clove garlic
1 Tbsp miso paste
2 tsp grated fresh ginger
1 Tbsp maple syrup
juice of ½ lime
1 tsp salt
1 tsp freshly ground black pepper

METHOD

Place all ingredients in a food processor and process until well combined. Transfer to a bowl and serve. Store in an airtight container in the refrigerator for up to one week.

Makes 2½ cups

CASHEW & CAPSICUM DIP

INGREDIENTS

1 cup (135g/4.8oz) cashews
1 red capsicum, chopped
2 Tbsp maple syrup
1 tsp Himalayan sea salt
1 tsp freshly ground black pepper
½ cup (125ml) extra virgin olive oil
1 tsp smoked paprika
Maple Baby Carrots (see page 134), to serve

METHOD

Place all ingredients in a high-speed blender and blend on low until smooth. Pour into a serving jar and serve with Maple Baby Carrots.

Makes 1½ cups

PECAN PÂTÉ

INGREDIENTS

2 cups (270g/9.6oz) pecans, soaked (see page 15)
¼ cup (63ml) extra virgin olive oil
3 Tbsp agave nectar
3 Tbsp tamari
½ tsp Himalayan sea salt
pinch of freshly ground black pepper

METHOD

Place all ingredients in a food processor and process on low, scraping down the sides occasionally until the mixture has fully combined. Can be used for the Green Apple & Pecan Pâté Canapé (see page 141). Store in an airtight container, refrigerated, for up to four weeks.

Makes 3 cups

ROSEMARY OREGANO PESTO

INGREDIENTS

1 cup (160g/5.6oz) **almonds**, soaked (see page 15)

½ cup (125ml) **extra virgin olive oil**

½ cup (10g/0.4oz) **rosemary leaves**

½ cup (10g/0.4oz) **oregano leaves**

2 tsp **Himalayan sea salt**

1 tsp **freshly ground black pepper**

METHOD

Place the almonds and olive oil in a high-speed blender and blend until smooth. Add the rest of the ingredients and blend again, stirring occasionally to make sure all ingredients are well mixed. Serve in a bowl or store in an airtight container, refrigerated, for up to two weeks.

Makes 2 cups

TIP

This pesto is a great staple to have in the fridge for dipping veges into, spreading on crackers or mixing through salads. We use this pesto at the café as the dressing for our Zucchini Noodle Salad.

FOCACCIA

Mum often made focaccia bread when I was growing up, and I loved the aroma of fresh rosemary wafting from the oven, so I wanted to create the same flavour and feeling with this raw version.

INGREDIENTS

2 cups (180g/6.4oz) **gluten-free oats**

2½ cups (315g/11oz) **dehydrated almond pulp** or 2 cups (200g/7oz) **almond meal**

⅔ cup (100g/3.8oz) **flaxmeal**

6 Tbsp **filtered water**

3 Tbsp **rice malt syrup**

3 Tbsp chopped **oregano leaves**

3 Tbsp **lemon juice**

¼ cup (45g/1.6oz) **pitted black olives**, sliced

fresh **rosemary leaves** (optional)

1 tsp **Himalayan sea salt**

METHOD

Place the gluten-free oats in a high-speed blender and blend on high until oats turn to powder. Set aside. If using dehydrated almond pulp, place in the blender and blend on high until a powder forms. Mix oats and almond pulp or meal with flaxmeal, filtered water, rice malt syrup, oregano and lemon juice.

Mix gently, using your hands, until a dough forms. Knead into a ball and then pat into your desired shape. I like to create the classic round shape with the dough about 5cm deep. Press olives firmly in to the top of the bread. Sprinkle with some rosemary leaves and sea salt. Place on a lined dehydrator tray and dehydrate for 12 hours. Store in an airtight container, refrigerated, for up to one week.

Makes 1 loaf

KALE CHIPS TWO WAYS

INGREDIENTS

6 cups **curly kale**, stalks removed

SMOKED PAPRIKA SAUCE
1 cup (135g/4.8oz) **cashews**, soaked (see page 12)

½ **red capsicum**

juice of 1 **lemon**

1 Tbsp **nutritional yeast**

1 Tbsp **rice malt syrup**

1 Tbsp **sweet smoked paprika**

1 drop **liquid smoke**

THYME & CHEDDAR SAUCE
1 cup (135g/4.8oz) **macadamias**, soaked (see page 15)

juice of 1 **lemon**

1 Tbsp **nutritional yeast**

1 Tbsp **rice malt syrup**

½ tsp **turmeric**

½ tsp **salt**

1 Tbsp **thyme leaves**

METHOD

Roughly chop kale into chip-sized pieces. Set aside. Place all sauce ingredients of your choice in a high-speed blender and blend until smooth. You may need to stop the blender occasionally and scrape down the sides to make sure all ingredients are combined. Pour the sauce over the kale and use your hands to massage in. Place the kale onto lined dehydrator trays and dehydrate for 8 hours. Store kale chips in a dry airtight container in a cupboard.

Makes 5 cups

CUCUMBER ROLLS

INGREDIENTS

ALMOND FETA
(MAKES 1½ CUPS)
1 cup (160g/5.6oz) almonds, soaked (see page 15)
¼ cup (63ml) lemon juice
3 Tbsp extra virgin olive oil
1 clove garlic
1 tsp Himalayan sea salt

CUCUMBER ROLLS
1 telegraph cucumber
2 cups (510g/18oz) Almond Feta
1 cup alfalfa sprouts

GARNISH
3 Tbsp black sesame seeds

METHOD

To make the almond feta, place all ingredients in a high-speed blender and blend until smooth and well combined. Set aside.

To make the cucumber rolls, trim the top and bottom from the cucumber and discard. Cut the cucumber in half and, using a mandolin or a sharp knife, cut lengthways into very thin slices. Lay a slice of cucumber down and place a tablespoonful of almond feta in the centre, add a tablespoon of alfalfa sprouts on top. Starting from one end, roll the cucumber around the almond feta and sprouts. Push a toothpick through the roll to keep it in place. Transfer each roll onto a platter as you go. Once all the cucumber slices have been used, garnish the rolls with sesame seeds. Cucumber rolls can be stored in an airtight container for up to three days.

Makes 30

TIP

These rolls are so quick and easy to prepare and a crowd-pleasing, healthy option to take to a pot luck dinner. Or make them as nibbles for your guests at your next dinner party.

MAPLE BABY CARROTS

INGREDIENTS

1 clove **garlic**
1 thumb **fresh ginger**
3 Tbsp **maple syrup**
⅓ cup (83ml) **tamari**
3 Tbsp **extra virgin olive oil**
25 **baby carrots**
1 cup **Cashew & Capsicum Dip**
(optional, see page 126)

METHOD

Place all ingredients except carrots in a high-speed blender and blend until smooth. Place the carrots in a shallow dish or container, pour the mixture over them and massage with your hands. Leave to marinate for at least 3 hours. Serve on their own or with Cashew & Capsicum Dip. Store, refrigerated, for up to one week.

TIP

These little carrots are wonderful for snacking on — they're nutritious and taste amazing! They're also great for entertaining and kids love them. I usually make up a batch on Sunday and leave them soaking throughout the week in the fridge. You don't need to use baby carrots in this recipe; you can use carrot sticks or celery.

CHEDDAR STICKS

INGREDIENTS

2 cups (250g/8.8oz) **dehydrated almond pulp** or **almond flour**

1½ cups (205g/7.2oz) **cashews**

½ cup (125ml) **extra virgin olive oil**

2 Tbsp **nutritional yeast**

2 Tbsp **rice malt syrup**

1 tsp **salt**

½ tsp **freshly ground black pepper**

1 clove **garlic**

2 Tbsp **flaxseeds**

⅓ cup (83ml) **filtered water**

METHOD

Slowly add all ingredients to the bowl of a food processor while processing on a low speed. Once the mixture begins to stick together, pulse to keep it moving around the bowl. Once the mixture is sticky and well blended, use your hands to roll into a large ball.

Place the ball on a piece of baking paper the size of the dehydrator tray. Lay another piece of baking paper on top and use a rolling pin to flatten the dough into a square, about 2–3cm deep. Remove the top piece of baking paper and use a knife to lightly mark out cheese-stick lengths (about 12cm long by 2cm wide). Dehydrate for 8 hours.

After dehydration, refrigerate for 1 hour to set. Snap the sticks along the marked lines. Store, refrigerated, in an airtight container for up to two weeks.

Makes 12

BLACK SESAME CRACKERS

INGREDIENTS

3 cups (480g/16.8oz) flaxmeal

½ cup (75g/2.6oz) black sesame seeds

2 cups (280g/9.8oz) sunflower seeds

½ cup (125ml) extra virgin olive oil

¼ cup (63ml) tamari

2 Tbsp maple syrup

1 tsp Himalayan sea salt

1 tsp freshly ground black pepper

2 Tbsp dried thyme and/or rosemary

½ cup (125ml) filtered water

1 capsule activated charcoal (optional)

METHOD

Place all ingredients in a food processor and process on medium for 2 minutes, or until smooth. You will need to stop the food processor occasionally and scrape down the sides. Once smooth, spread onto a lined dehydrator tray with a pallet knife until 0.5cm deep. Mark lightly with a sharp knife into squares. Place on a dehydrator tray and dehydrate for 8 hours. Rest crackers in the fridge for 1 hour after dehydrating. Snap crackers along marked lines. Store in airtight container for up to four weeks.

Makes 30 crackers

TIP

Activated charcoal is a black powder that is used to absorb impurities and detoxify the digestive system. I love using activated charcoal in my dishes, as it adds a great depth of colour, doesn't change the flavour, and creates an interesting element to the dish. I often have an activated charcoal capsule or two first thing in the morning, if doing a juice cleanse, to help kickstart the detoxification process. You can buy activated charcoal in powder or capsule form from your local health food store, pharmacy or online.

CANAPÉ TOPPINGS

EDAMAME GUACAMOLE & SAUERKRAUT

INGREDIENTS

10 **Black Sesame Crackers** (see page 138) or crackers of your choice
10 tsp **Edamame Guacamole** (see page 124)
10 Tbsp **Sauerkraut** (see page 236)
pinch of **freshly ground black pepper**
microherbs, to garnish

METHOD

Arrange the crackers on a tray. Place a teaspoonful of Edamame Guacamole on each cracker and spread to the edges. Top with a tablespoonful of Sauerkraut. Garnish with a pinch of pepper and microherbs.

GREEN APPLE & PECAN PÂTÉ

INGREDIENTS

METHOD

10 Black Sesame Crackers
(see page 138) or crackers of
your choice

2 green apples

1 cup (250g/8.8oz) Pecan Pâté
(see page 126)

3 Tbsp extra virgin olive oil,
to garnish

Arrange the crackers on a tray and set aside. Halve the apples, cutting along the core. Hold the flat core side of the apple half and use a mandolin or sharp knife to cut the apple into very thin slices. Repeat with the other apple halves. Cut the slices into quarters or to your preferred shape. Place a tablespoonful of Pecan Pâté on each cracker and spread to the edges. Top with the apple quarters and arrange in a fan-like shape. Garnish with a drizzle of the extra virgin olive oil.

PEAR, ROCKET & CASHEW CHEESE

INGREDIENTS

METHOD

10 Black Sesame Crackers
(see page 138) or crackers of
your choice

2 pears

½ cup (125g/4.4oz) Quick Cheese
(see page 94)

1 cup (20g/0.7oz) rocket leaves

5 Tbsp balsamic vinegar,
to garnish

Arrange the crackers on a tray and set aside. Halve the pears, cutting along the core. Hold the flat core side of the pear half and use a mandolin or sharp knife to cut the pear into very thin slices. Repeat with the other pear halves. Cut the slices into quarters or to your preferred shape. Place a tablespoonful of Quick Cheese on each cracker and spread to the edges. Top with the pear quarters and arrange in a fan-like shape. Place rocket leaves on top of the pear. Garnish with a drizzle of the balsamic vinegar.

CAKES & TARTS

CAKES & TARTS

STRAWBERRY, LEMON & LIME CAKE

INGREDIENTS

BASE
1 cup (140g/4.9oz) sunflower seeds

1 cup (100g/3.5oz) desiccated coconut

1 tsp Himalayan sea salt

3 Tbsp coconut oil

1 cup (160g/5.6oz) dates, soaked for 4 hours

LEMON & LIME FILLING
1½ cups (205g/7.2oz) cashews

½ cup (125ml) coconut oil

2 cups (500ml) filtered water

1 cup (160g/5.6oz) dates

juice of 2 limes

juice of 3 lemons

1 tsp Himalayan sea salt

½ tsp vanilla bean powder

1 Tbsp psyllium husk powder

STRAWBERRY FILLING
1½ cups (205g/7.2oz) cashews

1 cup (200g/7oz) chopped strawberries

½ cup (125ml) coconut oil

⅔ cup (200/7oz) rice malt syrup

2½ cups (625ml) filtered water

1 tsp Himalayan sea salt

⅓ cup (50g/1.7oz) chopped beetroot

½ tsp vanilla bean powder

1 Tbsp psyllium husk powder

TO DECORATE
⅓ cup (45g/1.5oz) pistachios, chopped

⅓ cup (8g/0.3oz) freeze-dried raspberries

METHOD

To make the base, place sunflower seeds, desiccated coconut and sea salt in a food processor and process until fine. Add the coconut oil and process again until well mixed. Add the dates and process until mixture is smooth. Line a 22cm springform cake tin with baking paper. Press the mixture into the lined tin. Use the back of a spoon to press the mixture down, making sure that it is flat and level. Set aside.

To make the lemon & lime filling, place cashews, coconut oil, filtered water, dates, juices, sea salt and vanilla bean powder in a high-speed blender and blend until smooth. Add psyllium husk powder and briefly blend again to mix. Pour onto the base, smoothing it out so that it is flat and level (work quickly as psyllium will set the mixture). Refrigerate while making the next filling.

To make the strawberry filling, place cashews, strawberries, coconut oil, rice malt syrup, filtered water, sea salt, beetroot and vanilla bean powder in a high-speed blender and blend until smooth. Add psyllium husk powder and briefly blend again to mix. Pour the strawberry filling carefully on top of the lemon filling, again smoothing it out so that it is flat and level.

Decorate with pistachios and freeze-dried raspberries. Freeze for 8 hours to set. Remove cake from the tin while still frozen. It will last up to 8 hours once taken out of the freezer. Store this cake, refrigerated, in an airtight container for up to one week.

Makes one 22cm cake

CRUNCHY CHOC, HAZELNUT & CARAMEL CAKE

INGREDIENTS

BASE
1 cup (160g/5.6oz) almonds
1 cup (100g/3.5oz) desiccated coconut
½ cup (70g/2.5oz) cacao nibs
3 Tbsp raw cacao powder
½ cup (125ml) coconut oil
½ cup (150g/5.3oz) rice malt syrup
½ tsp Himalayan sea salt
½ tsp vanilla bean powder

HAZELNUT FILLING
1½ cups (205g/7.2oz) cashews
1½ cups (190g/6.6oz) hazelnuts
1½ cups (240g/8.4oz) dates
3 cups (750ml) filtered water
1 cup (250ml) coconut oil
½ tsp vanilla bean powder
½ tsp Himalayan sea salt
½ cup (120g/4.2oz) Irish Moss Paste (see page 36)

CARAMEL
2 cups (320g/11.2oz) dates, soaked for 4 hours
½ cup (125ml) filtered water
3 Tbsp coconut oil
1 tsp vanilla bean powder
1 tsp Himalayan sea salt

CHOCOLATE SAUCE
½ cup (125ml) coconut oil
½ cup (55g/2oz) raw cacao powder
½ cup (150g/5.3oz) rice malt syrup

GARNISH
½ cup (63g/2.2oz) hazelnuts, chopped

METHOD

To make the base, place almonds, coconut, cacao nibs and raw cacao powder in the food processor and process until fine. Add coconut oil and process again until coconut oil is well mixed. Add rice malt syrup, sea salt and vanilla bean powder and process until smooth. Line a 22cm springform cake tin with baking paper. Press the mixture into the lined tin. Use the back of a spoon to press the mixture down, making sure that it is flat and level.

To make the hazelnut filling, place cashews, hazelnuts, dates and filtered water in a high-speed blender and blend until smooth. Add coconut oil, vanilla bean powder and sea salt and blend again. Add Irish Moss Paste and blend again until well combined. Pour filling onto the base.

To make the caramel, place dates and filtered water in a high-speed blender and blend until smooth, occasionally scraping down the sides. Add the remaining ingredients and blend again until smooth. Place dollops of the caramel on top of the hazelnut filling. Use a spoon to press the caramel down into the centre of the cake, mixing gently so the caramel is swirled around.

Freeze for 8 hours. Remove cake from the tin while still frozen.

To make the chocolate sauce, place all ingredients in a high-speed blender and blend on slow until combined. Pour the chocolate sauce gently over the cake, pouring around the edges so that the chocolate drips down the sides. While the chocolate is still soft, sprinkle hazelnuts on top.

Refrigerate for 1 hour to set, then cut and serve. Store this cake, refrigerated, in an airtight container for up to one week. Alternatively, it can be stored in the freezer for up to three months.

Makes one 22cm cake

WHITE CHOCOLATE CAKE WITH FIG

INGREDIENTS

BASE
1 cup (140g/4.9oz) Brazil nuts

1 cup (100g/3.5oz) desiccated coconut

zest and juice of 1 orange

3 Tbsp coconut oil

pinch of vanilla bean powder

1 cup (160g/5.6oz) dates, soaked for 4 hours

WHITE CHOCOLATE FILLING
2 cups (270g/9.6oz) macadamias, soaked (see page 15)

2 cups (270g/9.6oz) cashews, soaked (see page 12)

1 cup (250ml) coconut oil

½ cup (125ml) cacao butter

2 cups (500ml) coconut milk

1½ cups (450g/15.9oz) rice malt syrup

1 cup (250ml) filtered water

3 Tbsp lucuma powder

1½ tsp salt

2 tsp vanilla bean powder

½ cup (120g/4.2oz) Irish Moss Paste (see page 36) or 2 Tbsp psyllium husk powder

COCONUT ICING
1 cup (260g/9.1oz) Vanilla Cashew Yoghurt (see page 244) or coconut yoghurt

½ cup (37.5g/1.3oz) coconut chips or threads

¼ cup (75g/2.6oz) rice malt syrup

TO DECORATE
2 figs

METHOD

To make the base, place Brazil nuts and coconut in the food processor and process until fine. Add orange zest and juice, coconut oil and vanilla bean powder and process again until thoroughly mixed. Add dates and process until smooth. Line a 22cm springform cake tin with baking paper. Press the mixture into the lined tin. Use the back of a spoon to press the mixture down firmly. Refrigerate.

To make the white chocolate filling, place macadamias, cashews, coconut oil, cacao butter, coconut milk, rice malt syrup and filtered water in a high-speed blender and blend on high until smooth. Add lucuma powder, salt and vanilla bean powder and blend again. Add Irish Moss Paste or psyllium husk powder and blend, making sure the mixture is smooth. Pour filling onto the base and freeze for 8 hours. Remove cake from the tin while still frozen.

To make the coconut icing, mix all icing ingredients in a bowl until thoroughly combined. Spread icing carefully over the top of the cake and decorate with figs. Store this cake, refrigerated, in an airtight container for up to one week. Alternatively, it can be stored in the freezer for up to three months.

Makes one 22cm cake

CHOCOLATE, VANILLA & BOYSENBERRY GÂTEAU

INGREDIENTS

BASE
1 cup (140g/4.9oz) sunflower seeds
1 cup (100g/3.5oz) coconut chips
1 tsp Himalayan sea salt
1 tsp vanilla bean powder
3 Tbsp coconut oil
1 cup (160g/5.6oz) dates

CHOCOLATE GÂTEAU
3 cups (405g/14.4oz) cashews
1 cup (250ml) filtered water
1 cup (110g/3.9oz) raw cacao powder
1 cup (160g/5.6oz) dates
1 tsp vanilla bean powder
1 tsp Himalayan sea salt
½ cup (150g/5.3oz) rice malt syrup
1 cup (250ml) coconut oil
3 Tbsp psyllium husk powder

VANILLA CREAM
2½ cups (340g/12oz) cashews
1 cup (250ml) coconut cream
½ cup (125ml) coconut oil
½ cup (150g/5.3oz) rice malt syrup
1 tsp vanilla bean powder

TO DECORATE
1 cup (130g/4.6oz) boysenberries
½ cup (100g/3.5oz) hulled strawberries, sliced

METHOD

To make the base, place sunflower seeds, coconut chips, sea salt and vanilla bean powder in food processor and process until fine. Add coconut oil and process until well mixed. Add dates and process until sticky. Line three 22cm springform cake tins with baking paper. Press into the first springform tin and press base flat with the back of a spoon. Refrigerate.

To make the chocolate gâteau, place cashews, filtered water, raw cacao powder, dates, vanilla bean powder, sea salt and rice malt syrup in a high-speed blender and blend until smooth. Add coconut oil and blend until creamy. Add psyllium husk powder and blend briefly to mix. Pour one third of the mixture onto the base (work quickly as psyllium will set the mixture). Pour another third in each of the other two springform tins. Spread the mixture, making sure it's flat and level, and freeze for 8 hours.

To make the vanilla cream, place all ingredients in a high-speed blender and blend gently until peaks start to form. Add more cashews if it's too runny.

Remove gâteau layers from their tins. Spread vanilla cream about 1cm thick onto first and second frozen gâteau layers. Decorate each layer with boysenberries, making sure there is even spacing between each berry (this is important to hold up the layers). Place second layer on top of first layer and third layer on top. Decorate top of gâteau with strawberries and any extra berries.

You may like to serve the gâteau with Vanilla Cashew Yoghurt (see page 244). Store, refrigerated, for up to three days. Alternatively, it can be stored in the freezer for up to two months.

Makes one 22cm cake

STRAWBERRY & RHUBARB GALETTE

INGREDIENTS

FILLING
1 cup (200g/7oz) chopped strawberries
2 rhubarb stalks, chopped
1 cup (200g/7oz) coconut sugar
½ cup (125ml) filtered water
½ tsp vanilla bean powder

PASTRY
2 cups (180g/6.4oz) gluten-free oats
2 cups (270g/9.6oz) cashews
3 Tbsp maple syrup
3 Tbsp filtered water
½ tsp vanilla bean powder
pinch of Himalayan sea salt

TO SERVE
Vanilla Cashew Yoghurt
(see page 244)

METHOD

To make the filling, mix strawberries, rhubarb, coconut sugar, filtered water and vanilla bean powder together in a bowl. Leave to soak while you make the pastry.

To make the pastry, place oats in a high-speed blender and blend until fine. Do the same for the cashews. Place all pastry ingredients in a food processor and process until a dough forms. Using your hands, roll the dough into a ball. Lay a piece of baking paper on the bench and place the dough on top. Cover with another piece of baking paper. Using a rolling pin, roll the dough flat (about 0.5cm). Remove the top layer of paper.

Drain the strawberry and rhubarb and place in the centre of the rolled-out dough. Carefully fold up the edges over the fruit and place in the dehydrator for 4 hours. Serve with Vanilla Cashew Yoghurt.

Makes 2 small or 1 large galette

CARAMELISED APRICOT, MASCARPONE & THYME FLAN

INGREDIENTS

CARAMELISED APRICOT
1 Tbsp filtered water
3 Tbsp coconut sugar
1 tsp thyme leaves, plus extra
to garnish
pinch of Himalayan pink salt
10 apricots

PASTRY
1½ cups (135g/4.8oz) gluten-free
oats
1½ cups (205g/7.2oz) cashews
3 Tbsp coconut oil
1 tsp vanilla bean powder
⅓ cups (35g/1.3oz) raw cacao
powder
3 Tbsp rice malt syrup

MASCARPONE
flesh of 1 coconut or 1 cup
(135g/4.8oz) cashews
1½ cups (375ml) filtered water
½ cup (70/2.4oz) cashews
½ cup (150g/5.3oz) rice malt syrup
1 Tbsp lucuma powder
½ tsp vanilla bean powder
½ tsp Himalayan sea salt
½ cup (125ml) coconut oil
2 Tbsp Irish Moss Paste
(see page 36) or 1 Tbsp psyllium
husk powder

METHOD

To make the caramelised apricot, mix filtered water, coconut sugar, thyme and salt together in a bowl. Slice apricots into segments, removing tip and stone, and place in the bowl to marinate for 1 hour. Strain apricots and place on a lined dehydrator tray. Dehydrate for 2 hours.

To make the pastry, pulse oats in a high-speed blender until they are a fine powder. Place the oats in a mixing bowl. Blend the cashews until they also are a fine powder and add to the oats. Warm the coconut oil until liquid and add to the bowl along with the vanilla bean powder, raw cacao powder and rice malt syrup. Knead the mixture until it forms a dough. Line a 9.5 x 11.5 x 2.5cm rectangular tart tin with baking paper and press the dough into the tin, making sure to keep an even thickness (about 0.5cm). Dehydrate for 8 hours.

To make the mascarpone, place the coconut flesh/cashews, filtered water, cashews, rice malt syrup, lucuma powder, vanilla bean powder and sea salt in a high-speed blender and blend until creamy and smooth. Warm the coconut oil to liquid and pour into the blender. Blend again until well combined. Add the Irish Moss Paste or psyllium husk powder and blend until well combined. Pour the mascarpone on top of the pastry and refrigerate for 1 hour to set. Using Irish Moss Paste will create a light, fluffy texture, similar to mascarpone. If using psyllium husk powder, only refrigerate for 45 minutes. The psyllium will create a dense, firm texture, similar to cheesecake.

Once the mascarpone has set, place the caramelised apricots on top. Garnish with extra thyme leaves and serve. The flan can be stored, refrigerated, in an airtight container for up to one week. Alternatively, freeze for up to three months.

Makes one 9.5 x 11.5cm flan

EARL GREY & CARDAMOM TART WITH CARAMEL SAUCE

INGREDIENTS

BASE
1½ cups (135g/4.8oz) gluten-free oats
1½ cups (205g/7.2oz) cashews
3 Tbsp filtered water
3 Tbsp rice malt syrup
½ tsp vanilla bean powder
pinch of Himalayan sea salt

EARL GREY FILLING
2 cups (270g/9.6oz) cashews
1 cup (250ml) filtered water
⅔ cup (200g/7oz) rice malt syrup
½ cup (125ml) coconut oil
3 tsp Earl Grey loose leaf tea
½ tsp salt
½ tsp cardamom seeds
½ cup (120g/4.2oz) Irish Moss Paste (see page 36)

CARAMEL SAUCE
1 cup (160g/5.6oz) dates, soaked for 4 hours
1 Tbsp coconut oil
1 tsp Himalayan sea salt
pinch of vanilla bean powder

METHOD

To make the tart bases, place all base ingredients in a food processor. Process until a dough forms. Press the dough into three mini 10cm tart tins to a depth of 0.5cm. Place the tarts in the dehydrator and leave for 12 hours. Remove tart cases from tins and refrigerate until the filling is ready.

To make the Earl Grey filling, place all ingredients in a high-speed blender and blend until smooth and creamy. Pour filling into tart cases and refrigerate for 30 minutes to set.

To make the caramel sauce, place all sauce ingredients in a high-speed blender and blend on high, scraping down the sides occasionally, until the mixture resembles smooth caramel. Pour caramel into a squeezy bottle or piping bag (see Tip).

When tart is set, pipe caramel sauce on top to decorate. Tarts can be stored, refrigerated, in an airtight container for one week, but are best in the first three days.

Makes three 10cm tarts

TIP

To make your own piping bag, simply snip the corner off a small plastic bag, fill with icing/sauce and squeeze it through the small hole you have made.

LEMON CURD TARTS

INGREDIENTS

TART BASE
2 cups (200g/7oz) gluten-free oat flour

2 cups (140g/5oz) cashew flour

3 Tbsp filtered water

3 Tbsp rice malt syrup

½ tsp salt

½ tsp vanilla bean powder

1 Tbsp coconut sugar

LEMON CURD FILLING
flesh of 1 young coconut or ¾ cup (105g/3.6oz) cashews

½ cup (125ml) coconut oil

zest and juice of 5 lemons

½ cup (150g/5.3oz) rice malt syrup

½ cup (125ml) filtered water

½ tsp Himalayan sea salt

½ tsp vanilla bean powder

GARNISH
4 Tbsp coconut chips

METHOD

To make the tart bases, place all base ingredients in a food processor. Process until a dough forms. Press the dough into three mini 10cm tart tins to a depth of 0.5cm. Place the tarts in the dehydrator and leave for 12 hours. Remove tart cases from tins and refrigerate until the filling is ready.

To make the lemon curd filling, place all filling ingredients in a high-speed blender and blend until smooth and creamy. Pour into tart cases and refrigerate for 30 minutes until set.

Garnish the tarts with coconut chips. Place in an airtight container and refrigerate for up to three days.

Makes three 10cm tarts

MINI TIRAMISU

INGREDIENTS

BASE
1 cup (135g/4.8oz) cashews
1 cup (90g/3.2oz) gluten-free oats
1 tsp cinnamon
3 Tbsp coconut oil
½ cup (150g/5.3oz) coconut nectar
½ tsp vanilla bean powder

VANILLA LAYER
1 cup (135g/4.8oz) cashews
⅓ cup (83ml) coconut oil
1 cup (250ml) coconut milk
½ cup (150g/5.3oz) rice malt syrup
½ tsp vanilla bean powder
pinch of Himalayan sea salt
¼ cup (60g/2.1oz) Irish Moss Paste (see page 36)

COFFEE LAYER
1 cup (135g/4.8oz) cashews
½ cup (125ml) coconut oil
1 cup (250ml) cold-brew coffee
1 cup (160g/5.6oz) dates
½ tsp vanilla bean powder
pinch of Himalayan sea salt
¼ cup (60g/2.1oz) Irish Moss Paste (see page 36)

CHOCOLATE LAYER
1 cup (135g/4.8oz) cashews
½ cup (125ml) coconut oil
1 cup (250ml) filtered water
1 cup (160g/5.6oz) dates
½ tsp vanilla bean powder
pinch of Himalayan sea salt
¼ cup (60g/2.1oz) Irish Moss Paste (see page 36)

GARNISH
1 tsp ground cinnamon

METHOD

To make the base, place cashews, oats and cinnamon in a food processor and process until fine. Add coconut oil, coconut nectar and vanilla bean powder and blend until smooth. Press the mixture into four tall 7cm cake tins.

To make the vanilla layer, place all ingredients in a high-speed blender and blend until smooth. Pour evenly onto each base. Refrigerate while making the next layer.

To make the coffee layer, place all ingredients in the blender and blend until smooth. Carefully pour evenly on top of vanilla layer. Refrigerate while making the next layer.

To make the chocolate layer, place all ingredients in the blender and blend until smooth. Carefully pour evenly on top of coffee layer. Freeze for 8 hours.

Remove cakes from the tins and sprinkle with cinnamon. The cakes can be stored, refrigerated, for up to one week. Alternatively, they can be stored in the freezer for up to three months.

Makes four 7cm cakes

SPICED APPLE CARAMEL COBBLER

INGREDIENTS

BASE & TOPPING
1 cup (90g/3.2oz) **gluten-free oats**
1 cup (100g/3.5oz) **walnuts**
½ cup (85g/3oz) **sultanas**
5 Tbsp **coconut oil**
2 Tbsp **coconut sugar**
½ tsp **vanilla bean powder**
1 tsp **ground cinnamon**
1 tsp **ground ginger**
pinch of **ground cloves**
pinch of **ground nutmeg**

CARAMEL APPLE FILLING
3 **apples**, peeled and cored
1 cup (160g/5.6oz) **dates**, soaked for 4 hours
2 Tbsp **lemon juice**
1 tsp **vanilla bean powder**
1 tsp **Himalayan sea salt**

METHOD

To make the base and topping mixture, place oats and walnuts in a food processor and pulse until roughly chopped. Add the rest of the ingredients and process until well mixed. Halve the mixture and set half aside. Press half the mixture into the bottom of the cobbler pots or dishes.

To make the filling, cube the apples and set aside in a small bowl. Place the dates, lemon juice, vanilla bean powder and sea salt in a high-speed blender and blend until smooth. Pour into the bowl and use your hands to massage the caramel into the apple. Place the apple on top of the cobbler bases then top with the remaining half of the base/topping mixture. Press the mixture down so that it creates a hard layer. Dehydrate for 1 hour, to caramelise the top.

Serve immediately or store, refrigerated, in an airtight container for up to one week.

Serves 2

TIP

I usually make these little desserts in small cobbler pots (as pictured); if you don't have these, use a ceramic pot or dish, as you would for a home-made apple crumble. This dessert is warmed and slowly caramelised in the dehydrator, but you could also use the oven on a low heat with the door open.

COLD-BREW BROWNIE

INGREDIENTS

BASE & TOPPING
6 cups (750g/26.4oz) dehydrated almond pulp or almond flour
4 cups (360g/12.8oz) gluten-free oats
1 cup (110g/3.9oz) raw cacao powder
2 cups (500ml) coconut oil
½ tsp vanilla bean powder
1 tsp Himalayan sea salt
1 cup (300g/10.6oz) rice malt syrup
½ cup filtered water

COFFEE FILLING
2 cups (270g/9.6oz) cashews
½ cup (125ml) coconut oil
½ cup (150g/5.3oz) rice malt syrup
½ tsp salt
1 cup (250ml) cold-brew coffee
½ tsp vanilla bean powder
1 Tbsp psyllium husk powder

METHOD

Line a 25cm square springform cake tin with baking paper.

To make the base & topping, place almond pulp or flour and oats in a food processor and process until fine. Add the remaining ingredients and process until smooth. Set half the mixture aside. Press the other half of the mixture into the bottom of the cake tin. Use the back of a spoon to press the base down firmly and evenly.

To make the coffee filling, place cashews, coconut oil, rice malt syrup, salt, coffee and vanilla bean powder in a high-speed blender and blend on high until smooth. Add psyllium husk powder, blend briefly, and pour on top of base. Smooth out filling with the back of a spoon, making sure it is flat and level. Freeze for 6 hours.

Place the remaining half of the base & topping mixture on top of the filling. Press the mixture down so that it is firmly packed. Refrigerate for 1 hour to set.

Slice into about 20 pieces and serve. Store, refrigerated, in an airtight container for up to one week.

Makes one 25cm slice

STRAWBERRY, BEETROOT & CACAO SLICE

A nut-free raw slice!

INGREDIENTS

BASE
1 cup (100g/3.5oz) desiccated coconut
1 cup (140g/4.9oz) sunflower seeds
½ cup (55g/2oz) raw cacao powder
⅓ cup (83ml) coconut oil
½ tsp Himalayan sea salt
1 cup (160g/5.6oz) dates

STRAWBERRY LAYER
1½ cups (150g/5.3oz) desiccated coconut
2 cups (500ml) filtered water
½ cup (150g/5.3oz) rice malt syrup
1 cup (200g/7oz) hulled strawberries
½ cup (125ml) coconut oil
½ tsp vanilla bean powder
½ tsp Himalayan sea salt

BEETROOT LAYER
1½ cups (150g/5.3oz) desiccated coconut
2 cups (500ml) filtered water
½ cup (150g/5.3oz) rice malt syrup
½ cup (75g/2.6oz) beetroot, diced
½ cup (125ml) coconut oil
½ tsp vanilla bean powder
½ tsp Himalayan sea salt

CACAO LAYER
1 cup (100g/3.5oz) desiccated coconut
2 cups (500ml) filtered water
1 cup (160g/5.6oz) dates
½ cup (55g/2oz) raw cacao powder
½ cup (125ml) coconut oil
½ tsp vanilla bean powder
½ tsp Himalayan sea salt

METHOD

To make the base, place coconut and sunflower seeds in a food processor and process until fine. Add raw cacao powder, coconut oil and sea salt and blend until well combined. Add dates and blend until mixture is smooth. Line a 25cm square springform cake tin with baking paper and press the base mixture evenly into it.

To make the strawberry layer, place coconut and filtered water in high-speed blender and blend until smooth. Add the remaining ingredients and blend again until smooth. Pour onto the base, making sure that the mixture is flat and level. Refrigerate for 30 minutes to set before adding the next layer.

To make the beetroot layer, place coconut and water in the blender and blend until smooth. Add the remaining ingredients and blend again until smooth. Pour carefully onto the strawberry layer, making sure that the mixture is flat and level. Refrigerate for 30 minutes to set before adding the next layer.

To make the cacao layer, place coconut and water in the blender and blend until smooth. Add the remaining ingredients and blend again until smooth. Pour carefully onto the beetroot layer, making sure that the mixture is flat and level. Freeze for 8 hours.

Remove from the cake tin while slice is still frozen. Refrigerate for 45 minutes, then slice into about 20 pieces and serve. Store, refrigerated, in an airtight container for up to one week. Alternatively, store in the freezer for up to three months.

Makes one 25cm slice

SELF-LOVE

Once you start loving yourself, valuing your own time and listening to what serves you best, you begin to unravel a bigger love for yourself. Once you start respecting yourself, while being humble and kind to others, it really opens up a fresh perspective and happiness comes from small things.

There's nothing selfish about self-love. Making time for ourselves re-energises and restores a sense of peace and connectedness with ourselves. It also gives us the ability to take care of other people, really listen to others and be compassionate. It is important to reconnect.

TECHNOLOGY FAST
Go for a whole day without your phone, laptop or television. If you need these for work, then go a day without social media. Notice how much spare time you have. What will you do with that time?

GO TO A YOGA CLASS
Going to a yoga class can help relieve pressure, relax your mind and help you find an inner love that comes through presence and focusing on the 'now'. Go with a friend or by yourself and enjoy the feeling of stretching out your muscles. Think of the goodness it is doing to your body and mind.

DO SOMETHING YOU LOVE
Whether it be making food, exercising, looking at your favourite blogs, writing, drawing or listening to music. Whatever makes you happy, just do it and notice how you feel while you are doing this. Do it more often and see how it changes the way you feel about yourself.

MORNING ROUTINE
We as humans love routine. Doing the same thing every morning brings us a sense of peace, and we feel in control of our morning, which affects the rest of the day. Try getting up half an hour earlier to make yourself a nourishing breakfast, sit next to the window or outside, and do some stretching, meditation or affirmations. I love to do affirmations before I leave the house, as it allows me to reset my mind for the day, especially if there is a lot to do and people to meet. We can only be our best for other people when we feel good within ourselves. Having a moment to set your day up determines your approach to the rest of the day. It's a small change for a big impact.

BUY A JOURNAL AND WRITE IN IT
Writing is a way of getting everything down on paper that might be floating around in our minds, whether it's a 'to do' list or a creative story. I often like to make a list of the goals I am working on, or some creative ideas that are bouncing around, in order to release some clutter and help me bring my mind to the present.

GIVE YOURSELF A FACIAL
Spending a Saturday night in with a good book and a nourishing face mask is a great way to reset and re-energise yourself. Get into your favourite comfy clothes, make a pot of tea and enjoy the feeling of alone time. See how to make your own face mask on the next page.

TAKE A BATH WITH ROSE PETALS AND COCONUT OIL
Light some candles and soak in an aromatic hot bath. It's especially wonderful after a long day at work or on a cold winter's evening.

TAKE A WALK IN NATURE
Nature is the best medicine sometimes. The feeling of fresh, clean air and being surrounded by beautiful trees can uplift us and give us the 'earthing' energy that we need to rebalance.

TAKE YOURSELF OUT FOR LUNCH
Treating yourself to your favourite meal for lunch can be a great way to re-energise and get back in sync with yourself, especially if you are able to escape a busy day for some down time. Take your favourite magazine or just enjoy your surroundings. Take in the atmosphere and watch the passers-by.

BODY CARE

What we put on the outside of the body is just as important as what we put inside. If we are going to change the way we eat to feel better, the same goes for what we put on our skin. Skin is our largest organ; it absorbs the creams, oils and make-up we use. What we put on our skin ends up in our bloodstream, and can end up wreaking havoc with our hormones. We are lucky that, these days, there is a huge selection of natural face and body products available that contain no harmful chemicals. It is important to be aware of what you are putting onto your skin, to read the labels and to ask questions if you are unsure.

I love making home-made creams, scrubs and oils so I know exactly what is in them, and it's so much more enjoyable using something you have made yourself! It is really fun to do with a friend or with the kids. It also allows you to try out what works best with your skin. I recommend researching which oils and herbs best suit your skin type, and adding them to these recipes.

COCONUT SUGAR BODY SCRUB

½ cup (100g/3.5oz) **coconut sugar**
⅓ cup (83ml) **coconut oil**
⅓ cup (30g/1.1oz) **gluten-free oats**
1 tsp **chai spice**

Place all ingredients in a small bowl and stir until well combined. Massage into your skin, starting at your legs and working your way up to your neck. Rinse off in the shower.

MATCHA FACE MASK

1 Tbsp **matcha powder**
1 Tbsp **raw honey**
flesh of ½ **avocado**
juice of 1 **lemon**

Place all ingredients in a small bowl and stir until well combined. Massage onto your face, using circular motions. Lie down and let the ingredients do the work. Leave on for 10 minutes, then wash off.

ROSE & ALOE BODY OIL

½ cup (125ml) **coconut oil**
¼ cup (30g/1.1oz) finely chopped **aloe vera flesh** (skin removed)
10 drops **rose essential oil**

Soften coconut oil so that it is not quite liquid, but easy to mash with a fork. Add aloe vera and rose oil. Massage into your skin. Store in an airtight container in a warm place for up to three days.

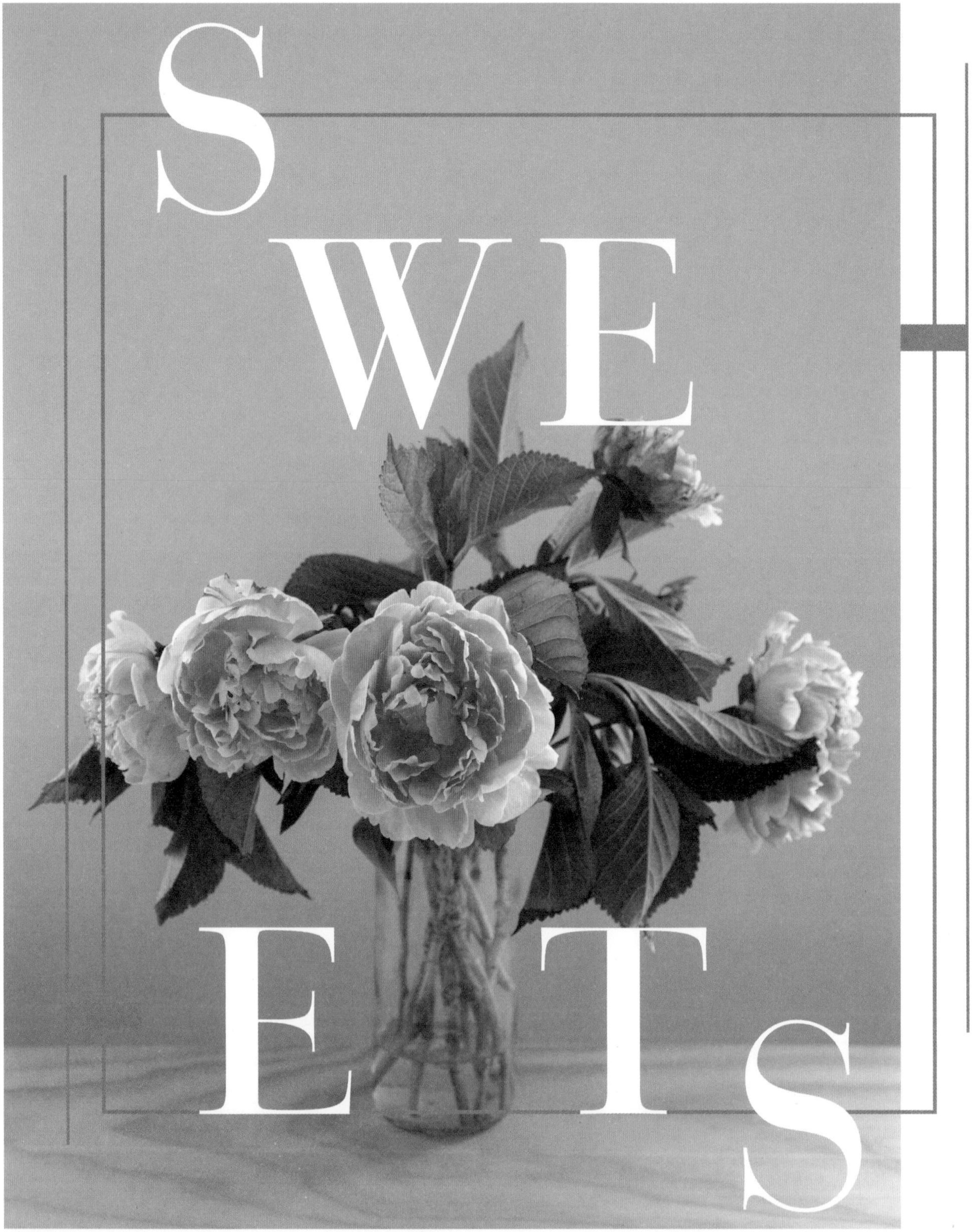
SWEETS

SWEETS

CARAMEL SLICE

INGREDIENTS

BASE
2 cups (180g/6.4oz) gluten-free oats
2 cups (270g/9.6oz) cashews
½ tsp Himalayan sea salt
3 Tbsp coconut oil
3 Tbsp rice malt syrup

CARAMEL FILLING
1 cup (250ml) coconut milk
3 Tbsp tahini
½ cup (150g/5.3oz) rice malt syrup
3 tsp vanilla bean powder
2 tsp Himalayan sea salt
1 cup (250ml) coconut oil
½ cup (125ml) cacao butter
1 cup (135g/4.8oz) cashews
3 cups (480g/16.8oz) dates, soaked for 4 hours

CHOCOLATE LAYER
½ cup (125ml) coconut oil
⅓ cup (35g/1.3oz) raw cacao powder
⅓ cup (100g/3.5oz) rice malt syrup
pinch of salt
pinch of vanilla bean powder

METHOD

To make the base, place the oats in a food processor and process until fine. Add the cashews and blend until fine. Add sea salt, coconut oil and rice malt syrup and blend on medium for 1 minute, until smooth. Line a 25cm square springform cake tin with baking paper and press the base mixture into it. Press with the back of a spoon to make sure it is flat and level. Refrigerate while you make the filling.

To make the filling, place coconut milk, tahini, rice malt syrup, vanilla bean powder, sea salt, coconut oil and cacao butter in a high-speed blender and blend on high for 2 minutes, until smooth. Add the cashews and blend on high for 2 minutes, until smooth. Add the soaked dates and blend again on high for 3 minutes, until smooth. Scrape down the sides of the blender if you need to and blend again to make sure all ingredients are incorporated. Pour filling onto the base, making sure it is evenly spread. Refrigerate again while you make the chocolate layer.

To make the chocolate layer, place all ingredients in the blender and blend slowly, on low, until combined. Do not process on high as this will cause ingredients to heat and separate. Pour onto the caramel filling slowly and evenly. Tip the cake tin on an angle slowly to make sure chocolate has covered all edges. Freeze for 8 hours. Remove from tin and allow to soften before cutting and serving.

Store, refrigerated, in an airtight container for up to one week.

Makes one 25cm slice

DONUTS

CARAMEL WITH WHITE CHOCOLATE SAUCE

INGREDIENTS

4 cups (400g/14oz) desiccated coconut, plus extra to garnish
2 cups (320/11.2oz) almonds
1 tsp Himalayan sea salt
1 tsp vanilla bean powder
½ cup (150g/5.3oz) maple syrup
1 cup (250ml) coconut oil
1 cup (160g/5.6oz) dates

WHITE CHOCOLATE SAUCE
½ cup (125ml) cacao butter
½ cup (150g/5.3oz) rice malt syrup
1 Tbsp mesquite powder (optional)
pinch of vanilla bean powder
pinch of Himalayan sea salt

METHOD

Place the coconut, almonds, sea salt, vanilla bean powder and maple syrup in a food processor and process on high for 2 minutes, until smooth. Add coconut oil and blend on medium for 1 minute. Add dates and blend until smooth. Spoon the mixture into a donut mould. Press down firmly so the mixture is tightly packed. Place the donut mould face down on the dehydrator tray and carefully press the donut out. Repeat until all mixture has been used and you've made about 10 donuts. Dehydrate for 8 hours, then refrigerate for 1 hour to set.

To make the white chocolate sauce, place all sauce ingredients in a high-speed blender and blend on slow for 30 seconds, until well combined. Do not blend on high as ingredients will heat and separate.

Pour sauce into a squeezy bottle (optional) and drizzle over donuts. Garnish with the extra desiccated coconut. Refrigerate for 20 minutes to set. Store, refrigerated, in an airtight container for up to three weeks.

Makes 10 donuts

CHILLI CHOCOLATE
WITH CHOCOLATE SAUCE

INGREDIENTS

4 cups (400g/14oz) desiccated coconut

2 cups (320g/11.2oz) almonds

1 tsp Himalayan sea salt

½ cup (55g/2oz) raw cacao powder

1 tsp cayenne pepper

½ tsp vanilla bean powder

½ cup (150g/5.3oz) maple syrup

1 cup (250ml) coconut oil

1 cup (160g/5.6oz) dates

CHOCOLATE SAUCE

½ cup (125ml) coconut oil

½ cup (150g/5.3oz) rice malt syrup

3 Tbsp raw cacao powder

pinch of vanilla bean powder

pinch of Himalayan sea salt

GARNISH

2 tsp ground chilli flakes

METHOD

Place the coconut, almonds, sea salt, cacao powder, cayenne pepper, vanilla bean powder and maple syrup in a food processor and process on high for 2 minutes, until smooth. Add coconut oil and blend on medium for 1 minute. Add dates and blend until smooth. Spoon the mixture into a donut mould. Press down firmly so the mixture is tightly packed. Place the donut mould face down on the dehydrator tray and carefully press the donut out. Repeat until all mixture has been used and you've made about 10 donuts. Dehydrate for 8 hours, then refrigerate for 1 hour to set.

To make the chocolate sauce, place all sauce ingredients in a high-speed blender and blend on slow for 30 seconds, until well combined. Do not blend on high as ingredients will heat and separate.

Pour sauce into a squeezy bottle (optional) and drizzle over donuts. Garnish with ground chilli flakes. Refrigerate for 20 minutes to set. Store, refrigerated, in an airtight container for up to three weeks.

Makes 10 donuts

STRAWBERRY & MACA WITH LUCUMA SAUCE

INGREDIENTS

4 cups (400g/ 14oz) desiccated coconut
2 cups (320g/11.2oz) almonds
1 tsp Himalayan sea salt
½ cup (150g/5.3oz) rice malt syrup
½ cup (12g/0.4oz) freeze-dried strawberries
½ tsp vanilla bean powder
1 Tbsp maca powder
1 cup (250ml) coconut oil

LUCUMA SAUCE
½ cup (125ml) coconut oil
½ cup (150g/5.3oz) rice malt syrup
3 Tbsp lucuma powder
pinch of vanilla bean powder
pinch of Himalayan sea salt

GARNISH
3 tbsp pistachio, chopped

METHOD

Place the coconut, almonds, sea salt, rice malt syrup , freeze-dried strawberries, vanilla bean powder and maca powder in a food processor and process on high for 2 minutes, until smooth. Add coconut oil and blend on medium until smooth. Spoon the mixture into a donut mould. Press down firmly so the mixture is tightly packed. Place the donut mould face down on the dehydrator tray and carefully press the donut out. Repeat until all mixture has been used and you've made about 10 donuts. Dehydrate for 8 hours, then refrigerate for 1 hour to set.

To make the lucuma sauce, place all sauce ingredients in a high-speed blender and blend on slow for 30 seconds, until well combined. Do not blend on high as ingredients will heat and separate.

Pour sauce into a squeezy bottle (optional) and drizzle over donuts. Garnish with chopped pistachio. Refrigerate for 20 minutes to set. Store, refrigerated, in an airtight container for up to three weeks.

Makes 10 donuts

ROSE CHOCOLATE

INGREDIENTS

1½ cups (375ml) coconut oil
1 cup (110g/3.9oz) raw cacao powder
1 cup (300g/10.6oz) rice malt syrup
½ tsp vanilla bean powder
½ tsp Himalayan sea salt
5–10 drops rose essential oil
2 Tbsp rose petals, to decorate

METHOD

Place all ingredients except rose petals in a high-speed blender and blend on low until smooth. Be careful not to over-blend, as this heats the chocolate and it will separate. Pour into a baking paper-lined 15–22cm square or rectangular cake tin. Decorate with rose petals. Refrigerate for 30 minutes to set. Remove the chocolate from the tin and place on a chopping board. Cut into 3cm squares and serve. Store, refrigerated, in an airtight container for up to four weeks.

Makes 30 pieces

TIP

If it's a hot day, the raw chocolate will go soft in the heat. Refrigerate to avoid a chocolatey mess!

CARAMEL CHOCOLATE

INGREDIENTS

2 cups (500ml) **coconut oil**
½ cup (150g/5.3oz) **maple syrup**
3 Tbsp **lucuma powder**
1 tsp **vanilla bean powder**
1 tsp **Himalayan sea salt**
3 Tbsp **pistachios**, to decorate

METHOD

Place the coconut oil and maple syrup in a high-speed blender and blend until smooth. Be careful not to over-blend, as this heats the chocolate and it will separate. Add the lucuma powder, vanilla bean powder and sea salt and blend until well combined. Pour into a baking paper-lined 15–22cm square or rectangular cake tin, making sure chocolate is flat and level. Decorate with pistachio nuts. Refrigerate for 30 minutes to set. Remove the chocolate from the tin and place on a chopping board. Cut into 3cm squares or break apart with your fingers. Store, refrigerated, in an airtight container for up to four weeks.

Makes 30 pieces

CARAMEL & WALNUT ICE CREAM

INGREDIENTS

flesh and water of 2 young Thai coconuts or 4 cups (1L) organic coconut cream

2 Tbsp coconut oil

1 cup (300g/10.6oz) rice malt syrup

2 Tbsp lucuma powder

1 tsp vanilla bean powder

1 tsp Himalayan sea salt

1 cup (100g/3.5oz) chopped Caramel Chocolate (see page 180)

⅔ cup (70g/2.4oz) walnuts, chopped

TO SERVE

maple syrup

⅓ cup (45g/1.5oz) chopped pistachios

METHOD

Place the coconut flesh and water or coconut cream, coconut oil, rice malt syrup, lucuma powder, vanilla bean powder and sea salt in a high-speed blender and blend until smooth. Stir in chopped caramel chocolate and walnuts.

USING FREEZER:
Pour into the ice cream mould (I usually use an old bread tin). Place in the freezer and stir frequently about every 30 minutes with a fork. Once the ice cream begins to set, leave it for 4 hours. Serve with a dollop of maple syrup and pistachios.

USING ICE CREAM MACHINE:
Pour into an ice cream machine and switch on. When ice cream machine has finished cooling and churning the ice cream (time varies for each machine), pour into an ice cream mould and place in the freezer. Serve with a dollop of maple syrup and pistachios.

Serves 4

RASPBERRY CLOUD PUFFS

INGREDIENTS

BASE
1 cup (135g/4.8oz) cashews
1 cup (90g/3.2oz) gluten-free oats
3 Tbsp coconut oil
3 Tbsp rice malt syrup
pinch of Himalayan sea salt

FILLING
12 tsp Berry Chia Jelly
(see page 39)
12 Tbsp Vanilla Cashew Yoghurt
(see page 244)

CHOCOLATE COATING
1 cup (250ml) coconut oil
1 cup (110g/3.9oz) raw cacao
powder
⅔ cup (200g/7oz) rice malt syrup
pinch of vanilla bean powder
pinch of Himalayan sea salt

GARNISH
⅓ cup (8g/0.3oz) freeze-dried
raspberries

METHOD

To make the base, place the cashews in a food processor and process on high until fine. Add the remaining ingredients and process on medium until mixture becomes sticky. Place a tablespoon of mixture into each of 12 mini silicone cupcake moulds, pressing down so that it is flat and level. Place a teaspoon of Berry Chia Jelly into each of the silicone moulds, pressing down with the back of the spoon but making sure the jelly doesn't reach the edges. Place a heaped tablespoon of Vanilla Cashew Yoghurt on top of the jelly, also making sure that the yoghurt doesn't reach the edges of the mould.

To make the chocolate coating, melt the coconut oil to liquid and place in a high-speed blender with the rest of the coating ingredients. Blend on low for 20 seconds. Be careful to not over-blend the chocolate, as it will separate. Pour the chocolate around the edges of each mould. Do not pour in the centre, directly on top of the yoghurt, as the chocolate will push the yoghurt down. When all moulds are filled, place onto a tray and refrigerate for 30 minutes to set. Garnish each puff with freeze-dried raspberries. Store, refrigerated, in an airtight container for up to two weeks.

Makes 12

MACAROONS

PASSIONFRUIT & BEE POLLEN

INGREDIENTS

3 cups (300g/10.5oz) desiccated coconut
½ cup (70g/2.4oz) macadamias
3 Tbsp rice malt syrup
5 Tbsp passionfruit pulp
1 Tbsp coconut oil
1 tsp bee pollen
½ tsp vanilla bean powder
½ tsp Himalayan sea salt

ICING
⅔ cup (90g/3.2oz) macadamias, soaked (see page 15)
⅓ cup (100g/3.5oz) rice malt syrup
⅓ cup (83ml) coconut oil

METHOD

Place the coconut and macadamias in a food processor and process until fine. Add the rest of the ingredients and process on medium for 3 minutes, until smooth. Be careful not to over-mix, as this will cause it to heat and separate.

Roll tablespoonfuls of the mixture into balls, then flatten with the palm of your hand. Place on a dehydrator tray and dehydrate for 6 hours.

To make the icing, place all ingredients in a high-speed blender and blend on high until smooth. Refrigerate to set for 45 minutes. Place a dollop of icing onto every second macaroon, then place the non-iced macaroons on top. Store, refrigerated, in an airtight container for up to two weeks.

Makes 8

RASPBERRY & ROSE

INGREDIENTS

3 cups (300g/10.5oz) desiccated coconut

½ cup (70g/2.4oz) macadamias

3 Tbsp rice malt syrup

1 Tbsp coconut oil

pinch of vanilla bean powder

½ tsp Himalayan sea salt

¼ cup freeze-dried raspberries

3 Tbsp filtered water

5–10 drops rose essential oil

ICING

⅔ cup (90g/3.2oz) macadamias, soaked (see page 15)

⅓ cup (100g/3.5oz) rice malt syrup

⅓ cup (83ml) coconut oil

METHOD

Place the coconut and macadamias in a food processor and process until fine. Add the rest of the ingredients and process on medium for 3 minutes, until smooth. Be careful not to over-mix, as this will cause it to heat and separate.

Roll tablespoonfuls of the mixture into balls, then flatten with the palm of your hand. Place on a dehydrator tray and dehydrate for 6 hours.

To make the icing, place all ingredients in a high-speed blender and blend on high until smooth. Refrigerate to set for 45 minutes. Place a dollop of icing onto every second macaroon, then place the non-iced macaroons on top. Store, refrigerated, in an airtight container for up to two weeks.

Makes 8

MINT & MATCHA

INGREDIENTS

3 cups (300g/10.5oz) desiccated coconut
½ cup (70g/2.4oz) macadamias
3 Tbsp rice malt syrup
1 Tbsp coconut oil
3 Tbsp filtered water
2 Tbsp matcha powder
5 drops peppermint essential oil
½ tsp vanilla bean powder
½ tsp Himalayan sea salt

ICING
⅔ cup (90g/3.2oz) macadamias, soaked (see page 15)
⅓ cup (100g/3.5oz) rice malt syrup
⅓ cup (83ml) coconut oil

METHOD

Place the coconut and macadamias in a food processor and process until fine. Add the rest of the ingredients and process on medium for 3 minutes, until smooth. Be careful not to over-mix, as this will cause it to heat and separate.

Roll tablespoonfuls of the mixture into balls, then flatten with the palm of your hand. Place on a dehydrator tray and dehydrate for 6 hours.

To make the icing, place all ingredients in a high-speed blender and blend on high until smooth. Refrigerate to set for 45 minutes. Place a dollop of icing onto every second macaroon, then place the non-iced macaroons on top. Store, refrigerated, in an airtight container for up to two weeks.

Makes 8

RASPBERRY & CHOCOLATE POP TARTS

INGREDIENTS

POP TARTS
1½ cups (135g/4.8oz) gluten-free oats
1½ cups (205g/7.2oz) cashews
⅓ cup (100g/3.5oz) maple syrup
pinch of vanilla bean powder
½ tsp Himalayan sea salt
8 Tbsp Berry Chia Jelly
(see page 39)

CHOCOLATE SAUCE
¼ cup (63ml) coconut oil
¼ cup (30g/1.1oz) raw cacao powder
¼ cup (75g/2.6oz) rice malt syrup

GARNISH
¼ cup (6g/0.2oz) freeze-dried raspberries

METHOD

To make the pop tarts, place oats and cashews in a high-speed blender and blend until flour-like. Place the oats and cashews, maple syrup, vanilla bean powder and sea salt in a food processor and process until a dough forms. Roll the dough into a ball. Lay a piece of baking paper on the bench and place the ball of dough on top. Place another piece of baking paper on top. Using a rolling pin, roll the dough flat.

Remove the top sheet of baking paper and cut the flattened dough into four 10cm squares. On two of the squares, place four dollops of Berry Chia Jelly. Carefully lift the other squares and place them on top of the jelly. Using a fork, gently press down the edges of the pop tart to seal the jelly inside. Dehydrate for 6 hours, then refrigerate for 30 minutes.

To make the chocolate sauce, warm the coconut oil and place in a small bowl. Add cacao powder and rice malt syrup and stir until creamy. Pour sauce into a small squeezy bottle and drizzle over pop tarts. While sauce is soft, garnish with freeze-dried raspberries.

Makes 2 pop tarts

WHITE CHOCOLATE, MACADAMIA & RASPBERRY POPSICLES

INGREDIENTS

½ cup (70g/2.4oz) macadamias
flesh and water of 1 Thai coconut
or 1 cup (250ml) organic coconut
cream
½ cup (150g/5.3oz) rice malt syrup
1 Tbsp vanilla bean powder
1 Tbsp coconut oil
2 Tbsp lucuma powder
6 Tbsp raspberry pulp

CHOCOLATE DIP
1 cup (250ml) coconut oil
½ cup (55g/2oz) raw cacao powder
½ cup (150g/5.3oz) rice malt syrup

TO DECORATE
¼ cup (40g/1.4oz) bee pollen

METHOD

Place the macadamias, coconut flesh and water or cream, rice malt syrup, vanilla bean powder, coconut oil and lucuma powder in a high-speed blender and blend until smooth. Place a tablespoon of raspberry pulp into each of six iceblock moulds and pour the blended mixture on top. Freeze for 1 hour, then place the sticks into the centre of the popsicles. Freeze for another 4 hours.

To make the chocolate dip, combine all ingredients in a high-speed blender and blend on a slow speed until well mixed. Pour the chocolate dip into a narrow glass. Take the popsicles out of the moulds. I usually do this by sitting the mould in a glass of hot water and pulling gently. Lay the popsicles on a baking paper-lined tray. Dip the popsicles halfway into the chocolate and return to the tray. Sprinkle with bee pollen, to decorate. Place the tray back into the freezer for the dip to set.

Makes 6

AFGHANS

INGREDIENTS

2 cups (320g/11.2oz) almonds
2 cups (270g/9.6oz) cashews
1 cup (110g/3.9oz) raw cacao powder
1 Tbsp tahini
½ cup (150g/5.3oz) maple syrup
½ cup (100g/3.5oz) coconut sugar
1 cup (150g/5.2oz) buckinis (optional)
1 tsp cinnamon
1 tsp vanilla bean powder
1 tsp Himalayan sea salt

ICING
1 cup (135g/4.8oz) cashews, soaked (see page 12)
½ cup (125ml) coconut oil
½ cup (150g/5.3oz) rice malt syrup, agave syrup or honey
½ cup (55g/2oz) raw cacao powder
½ tsp Himalayan sea salt
pinch of vanilla bean powder

TO DECORATE
½ cup (50g/1.8oz) walnut halves

METHOD

Place the almonds in a high-speed blender and blend until fine. Do the same with the cashews. Place the almonds and cashews in a food processor and add the remaining ingredients. Process until well mixed and sticky. Pour mixture into a bowl. Take three tablespoonfuls of mixture and roll into a ball. Place on a dehydrator tray and flatten with your hand or the back of a spoon. Repeat until all mixture has been used.

Dehydrate for 8 hours, then refrigerate.

To make the icing, place all ingredients in a high-speed blender and blend until smooth. Be careful not to over-blend, as the mixture will separate. Refrigerate to harden slightly, so it is easy to spread. Place a dollop of icing onto each afghan. Decorate with a walnut half and place back on the tray. Refrigerate for 1 hour to set icing.

These afghans can be stored in an airtight container for up to three weeks.

Makes 12

TIP

Buckinis are sprouted and dehydrated buckwheat, and create that crunchy element that cornflakes give in the traditional afghans. You can purchase buckinis from your local wholefoods store. You can make your own buckinis by soaking and dehydrating buckwheat. If you cannot source the buckinis, then don't worry – these cookies are still delicious without them! Maple syrup is really important in this recipe, as it gives the gooey, chewy texture that we love in traditional chocolate cookies. The kids will love them!

PISTACHIO & RASPBERRY BISCOTTI

These are a great low-sugar snack!

INGREDIENTS

1½ cups (205g/7.2oz) **cashews**
¼ cup (40g/1.4oz) **flaxseeds**
2 cups (180g/6.4oz) **gluten-free oats**
3 Tbsp **rice malt syrup**
½ cup (65g/2.3oz) **pistachios**
¼ cup (63ml) **filtered water**
¼ cup (63ml) **coconut oil**
¼ cup (50g/1.8oz) **coconut sugar**
½ tsp **vanilla bean powder**
½ tsp **Himalayan sea salt**

CHOCOLATE GLAZE
½ cup (150g/5.3oz) **rice malt syrup**
½ cup (55g/2oz) **raw cacao powder**
½ cup (125ml) **coconut oil**

TO DECORATE
½ cup (12g/0.4oz) **freeze-dried raspberries**

METHOD

Place the cashews in a high-speed blender, and blend until fine. Do the same with the flaxseeds and oats. Place the cashews, flaxseeds and oats in a food processor. Add rice malt syrup, pistachios, filtered water, coconut oil, coconut sugar, vanilla bean powder and sea salt. Process until a smooth dough forms.

Roll the dough into a ball. Lay a piece of baking paper on the bench and place the ball of dough on top. Place another piece of baking paper on top. Using a rolling pin, roll the dough into a rectangle, 2.5cm thick and about 10 x 20cm wide. Remove top piece of baking paper and, using a large knife, slice the biscotti into 2cm wide pieces. Dehydrate for 12 hours, then refrigerate for 1 hour.

To make the chocolate glaze, place all ingredients in a high-speed blender and blend on slow until well mixed. Do not over-blend as it will cause the mixture to heat and separate. Pour the chocolate glaze into a narrow cup or glass. Dip each biscotti halfway into the glaze, then return to the tray. Decorate with freeze-dried raspberries and refrigerate for 30 minutes to set. Store, refrigerated, in an airtight container for up to two weeks.

Makes 12

GINGER, CARAMEL & PISTACHIO COOKIES

INGREDIENTS

2 cups (270g/9.6oz) **cashews**
2 cups (180g/6.4oz) **gluten-free oats**
⅓ cup (100g/3.5oz) **maple syrup**
½ tsp **vanilla bean powder**
1 cup (130g/3.5oz) **walnuts**
1 tsp **salt**
3 Tbsp **ground ginger**
2cm piece **fresh ginger**, minced

CARAMEL SAUCE
1 cup (160g/5.6oz) **dates**, soaked for 4 hours
3 Tbsp **coconut oil**
½ tsp **vanilla bean powder**
1 tsp **Himalayan sea salt**

TO DECORATE
½ cup (65g/2.3oz) chopped **pistachios**

METHOD

Place all cookie ingredients in a food processor and process on medium until well mixed, sticky and pliable. Roll the mixture into a ball. Lay a piece of baking paper on the bench and place the ball on top. Place another piece of baking paper on top. Using a rolling pin, roll the mixture out so that it is 1cm thick. Cut into shapes using a cookie cutter. Gather up any trimmings and roll again, repeating the process until all the mixture is used up. Dehydrate cookies for 8 hours, then refrigerate for 1 hour.

To make the caramel sauce, place dates in a high-speed blender and blend until smooth. Add remaining ingredients and again blend until smooth and caramel-like. Pour the caramel sauce into a squeezy bottle and use to decorate the cookies. Sprinkle with chopped pistachios, and serve.

Store in an airtight container for up to three weeks.

Makes 18

RASPBERRY COCONUT O-BALLS

INGREDIENTS

1 cup (140g/4.9oz) sunflower seeds
1 cup (100g/3.5oz) desiccated coconut
⅓ cup (50g/1.7oz) chopped beetroot
⅓ cup (8g/0.3oz) freeze-dried raspberries
½ tsp Himalayan sea salt
½ tsp vanilla bean powder
3 Tbsp coconut oil
2 cups (320g/11.2oz) dates, soaked for 4 hours

COATING
1 cup (100g/3.5oz) desiccated coconut
¼ cup (6g/0.2oz) freeze-dried raspberries

METHOD

Place the sunflower seeds, desiccated coconut, beetroot, freeze-dried raspberries, sea salt and vanilla bean powder and blend until fine. Add the coconut oil and blend until well mixed. Add the dates and blend on low until well combined. Pour mixture into a bowl and set aside.

Place the desiccated coconut and freeze-dried raspberries in a small bowl and mix with your hands, rubbing to combine the raspberry colour with the coconut. Take two tablespoons of the mixture and roll into a ball. Place in the raspberry coconut mixture and roll around to coat completely. Continue to do this until you have used up all the mixture. Store, refrigerated, in an airtight container for up to three weeks.

Makes 12

DRINKS

DRINKS

CHAMOMILE CHOC MYLK

INGREDIENTS

1 cup (135g/4.8oz) cashews, soaked (see page 12)
10 pitted dates
5 Tbsp raw cacao powder
1 Tbsp chamomile tea
pinch vanilla bean powder
3⅔ cups (900ml) filtered water

METHOD

Place all ingredients in a high-speed blender and blend on high until smooth. Place a nut mylk bag (cheesecloth or muslin bag) in a bowl and pour the liquid into it. Strain the pulp out by squeezing it through the bag until there is only hard cashew pulp left. Pour mylk into a jug or jar and serve with ice.

Makes 1L

STRAWBERRIES & CREAM NUT MYLK

INGREDIENTS

1 cup (200g/7oz) hulled and chopped strawberrries
½ cup (50g/1.8oz) desiccated coconut, soaked
½ cup (80g/2.8oz) almonds, soaked
10g/0.35oz beetroot
⅓ cup (100g/3.5oz) rice malt syrup or sweetener of choice
pinch of vanilla bean powder
pinch of Himalayan sea salt
3⅔ cups (900ml) filtered water

METHOD

Place all ingredients in a high-speed blender and blend on high for 2–3 minutes until smooth. Place a nut mylk bag in a bowl and pour liquid into it. Strain the pulp out by squeezing it through the bag until there is only hard pulp left. Pour mylk into a jug or jar and serve with ice.

Makes 1L

CELEBRATION OF GREENS SMOOTHIE

INGREDIENTS

1 cup (220g/7.8oz) ice
1 cup (20g/0.7oz) chopped kale
1 cup (20g/0.7oz) chopped spinach
1 banana
½ pear, chopped
2 Tbsp desiccated coconut
1 tsp spirulina/greens powder
1 sprig parsley
1¾ cups (450ml) filtered water
pinch of bee pollen, to decorate

METHOD

Place all ingredients in a high-speed blender and blend on high until your preferred consistency is reached. Pour into a serving glass and decorate. I love using something bright like bee pollen.

Makes 500ml

TIP

Put the liquid in first. That way, the harder ingredients can be easily blended without getting stuck!

CACAO ALMOND SMOOTHIE

INGREDIENTS

1 cup (220g/7.8oz) ice
1 banana
5 dates
2 Tbsp almonds
1 Tbsp cacao nibs, plus extra
to serve
1 Tbsp cacao powder
1 tsp ground cinnamon
pinch of Himalayan sea salt
1⅔ cups (400ml) filtered water

METHOD

Place all ingredients in a high-speed blender and blend on high for 2–3 minutes until smooth. Pour into a serving glass and serve with a sprinkle of cacao nibs on top.

Makes 500ml

TIP

You may prefer to soak the almonds before using them in this recipe. This will ease the digestion and assimilation of nutrients. However, it's not necessary and will still taste delicious without!

GINGERBREAD SMOOTHIE

INGREDIENTS

1 cup (220g/7.8oz) ice

5 dates

½ pear, chopped

2 Tbsp cashews

1 thumb fresh ginger

1 tsp ground cinnamon

1 tsp vanilla bean powder

pinch of nutmeg

½ tsp cloves

1⅔ cups (400ml) Almond Mylk
(see page 234)

pinch of ground ginger, to garnish

METHOD

Place all ingredients in a high-speed blender and blend on high until your preferred consistency is reached. Pour into a serving glass and garnish with a pinch of ground ginger.

Makes 500ml

TIP

This creamy smoothie is one of my favourite breakfasts! It is warming, kick-starts the digestion and gives me plenty of energy to get through the morning. You can add a banana for an extra boost of flavour and energy.

GREEN ALKALISER SMOOTHIE

This one's for the serious green smoothie drinkers!

INGREDIENTS

½ cup (110g/3.9oz) **ice**
1 thumb **fresh ginger**
½ cup (75g/2.6oz) chopped
telegraph cucumber
3 Tbsp **lemon**
½ cup (10g/0.4oz) chopped
spinach
1 cup (20g/0.7oz) chopped **kale**
1⅔ cups (400ml) **filtered water**

METHOD

Place all ingredients, ice first, in a high-speed blender and blend on high for 2–3 minutes or until your preferred consistency is reached. Pour into a serving glass.

Makes 500ml

SALTED CARAMEL SMOOTHIE

Soaking the dates and cashews beforehand will give you a creamier consistency, but it's not necessary for a delicious drink!

INGREDIENTS

1 cup (220g/7.8oz) **ice**
1 **banana**
8 **dates**
2 Tbsp **cashews**
1 Tbsp **cacao nibs**, plus extra
to garnish
½ tsp **Himalayan sea salt**
pinch of **vanilla bean powder**
1¾ cups (450ml) **filtered water**
1 Tbsp chopped **pistachios**,
to garnish

METHOD

Place all ingredients in a high-speed blender and blend on high for 2–3 minutes until smooth or until your preferred consistency is reached. Pour into a large tumbler or Mason jar and garnish with some chopped pistachios.

Makes 500ml

DETOX HERBAL BLEND

INGREDIENTS

1 tsp **fennel seeds**

zest and **juice** of 1 **orange**

1 Tbsp **cacao nibs**

1 tsp **dried licorice root**

1 tsp **dried dandelion**

pinch of **vanilla bean powder**

2 cups (500ml) **boiling water**

METHOD

Place all ingredients in a tea strainer or teapot with a strainer attachment. Slowly pour over boiling water and leave to steep for 3 minutes. Remove leaves and serve. Leave to cool down to drinking temperature.

Makes 500ml

TIP

I like to drink my detox blend first thing in the morning, to stimulate the liver and get the detoxification process started. I also love to sip on this throughout the day, or while on a juice cleanse, as it has potent healing powers. The unique combination of ingredients in this blend has been formulated to enhance your body's natural detoxifying processes, helping to cleanse out lingering toxins and impurities. The licorice root and dandelion will help to soothe your digestion, providing a feeling of refreshment and vitality.

GINGER & ROSE KOMBUCHA

INGREDIENTS

4 cups (1L) filtered water

½ cup (115g/4oz) organic cane sugar

3 tsp rose water

4 black tea bags

2 Tbsp finely chopped ginger

1 kombucha SCOBY
(see page 14)

2 Tbsp organic dried roses, to serve

METHOD

Place the filtered water, sugar and rose water in a saucepan and bring to boil. Remove from the heat and add tea bags. Leave to cool down to room temperature, stir well, remove tea bags, and pour liquid into a sterilised glass jar and add ginger. Place the SCOBY in the jar and stir lightly. Place a clean cheese cloth or tea towel over the top of the jar, using a rubber band or string to secure it around the top. Place out of direct sunlight and leave for 3–5 days.

Remove the SCOBY from the kombucha. (You may restart the process or store the SCOBY in the fridge in a small jar with a small amount of kombucha.) Store the kombucha in the fridge in an airtight jar. The longer you leave it, the more it will ferment and the fizzier it will become. Serve the kombucha with dried roses.

Makes 1L

MATCHA MYLKSHAKE

An iced matcha is a great substitute for coffee on a warm summer's day. It will provide you with a natural energy boost.

INGREDIENTS

4 tsp **matcha powder**
2 cups (500ml) **Almond Mylk**
(see page 234)
pinch of **vanilla bean powder**
5 drops **stevia**
1 cup (220g/7.8oz) **ice**

METHOD

Place matcha powder in a serving jug. Slowly pour Almond Mylk into the jug, using a fork or small whisk to stir as you pour. Add vanilla bean powder and stevia and mix again. Place ½ cup of ice into each serving glass and pour the matcha on top. Serve immediately

Makes 500ml

STRAWBERRY & MINT KEFIR

INGREDIENTS

4 Tbsp **kefir grains**
4 cups (1L) **filtered water**
4 Tbsp **organic cane sugar**
1 cup (200g/7oz) sliced **strawberries**
3 sprigs of **mint**
1 **lemon**, sliced

METHOD

Strain and rinse kefir grains with clean water. Place water and sugar in a sterile 1L jar and stir until sugar dissolves. Place kefir grains in the jar and secure the lid. Leave in a warm room (I often leave mine on top of my dehydrator) for 24 hours, then give the mixture a good stir. The kefir will now be fizzy. You may want to leave for another 24 hours to become fizzier or if the room hasn't been warm enough it may take longer than 24 hours to become fizzy.

Strain out kefir grains and place the fizzy kefir in a new jar. Place strawberries in the kefir and crush with your hand to release the strawberry juice. This adds a nice colour to the kefir. Pour into glasses and serve with mint leaves and sliced lemon. Store leftover kefir in an airtight glass jar in the fridge. Use the leftover kefir grains to start a new batch of kefir or store in the fridge in water and sugar in an airtight jar.

Makes 1L

KEFIR ICE CREAM FLOAT

INGREDIENTS

3 cups (750ml) **Strawberry & Mint Kefir** (see page 220)

2 scoops **organic coconut ice cream**

sprig of **mint** or **edible flowers**, to serve

METHOD

Pour kefir into two large tumblers. Take a scoop of ice cream and carefully place in each tumbler. Serve with a sprig of mint or edible flowers.

Serve 2

LAVENDER & PEACH ICE TEA

This is the perfect summer drink for early evenings outside, entertaining friends, or just sitting by yourself with a good book. Refreshing and delicious!

INGREDIENTS

3 soft **peaches**, stone removed
3 cups (750ml) strained **black tea**, cooled to room temperature
2 tsp **dried lavender**
¼ cup (75g/2.6oz) **rice malt syrup**
juice of 1 **lemon**
pinch of **vanilla bean powder**
1 tsp **rose water** (optional)

TO SERVE
1 cup (220g/7.8oz) **ice**
sprig of **lavender**

METHOD

Dice the peaches and place in a high-speed blender with the black tea, dried lavender, rice malt syrup, lemon, vanilla and rose water, and blend until smooth. Pour into glass tumblers and serve with ice and a sprig of lavender.

Makes 750ml

TIP

You can use lavender that has been freshly picked from your garden. Just make sure it is free from animal urine and exposure to traffic toxins!

MAYAN HOT CHOCOLATE

This warming drink is delicious on wintery evenings. I love cuddling up with a good book and sipping on this slowly, as it has a kick of spice that warms your insides.

INGREDIENTS

½ cup (55g/2oz) raw cacao powder

3 cups (750ml) Almond Mylk
(see page 234)

1 Tbsp lucuma powder

10 dates, soaked for 4 hours

1 tsp maca powder

1 tsp ground cinnamon

1 tsp ground cardamom

½ tsp cayenne pepper

½ tsp Himalayan sea salt

1 tsp vanilla bean powder

grated nutmeg or dried chilli,
to serve

METHOD

Place all ingredients in a high-speed blender and blend until smooth. Pour into a saucepan and warm on the stove top or in a dehydrator, if preferred. Serve with a pinch of grated nutmeg or dried chilli on top.

Makes 750ml

TIP

In ancient times, raw cacao was used for healing purposes. The addition of lucuma powder adds a natural sweetness but with a low GI for a slow release of energy.

PEAR, CARROT & CINNAMON TONIC

INGREDIENTS

6 carrots

4 pears

1 tsp ground cinnamon

METHOD

Juice the carrot and pear and pour into a serving jug. Add the cinnamon and stir until well mixed. Pour into a glass tumbler and serve.

Makes 700ml

MACA BERRY BOMB

INGREDIENTS

1 cup (170g/6oz) frozen mixed berries

1 banana

1 Tbsp maca powder

5 dates

1¾ cups (450ml) filtered water

METHOD

Place all ingredients in a high-speed blender and blend until smooth. Serve in a 500ml glass.

Makes 500ml

GINGER & TURMERIC HEALTH ELIXIR

INGREDIENTS

½ cup (80g/2.8oz) fresh turmeric
¾ cup (120g/4.2oz) chopped
fresh ginger
1 Tbsp raw honey
pinch of Himalayan sea salt
⅓ cup (83ml) filtered water

METHOD

Juice the turmeric and ginger and place in a small bowl. Add the honey, sea salt and filtered water and stir until well mixed. Pour into a small glass tumbler and drink — enjoy the feeling of awakened senses!

Makes 1 cup

TIP

Whenever I go to Bali, I always pick up a bottle of 'Jamu' from my favourite raw food café, Alchemy. I love the strong kick of turmeric it gives. This is my version, with a delicious sweet hint of local raw honey. Have a shot of this juice when you are beginning to feel under the weather, and it will give you an immune boost that will help you get back on the right track.

PANTRY STAPLES

PANTRY STAPLES

THE RAW KITCHEN ALMOND MYLK

This mylk is a fresh and creamy substitute for traditional cow's milk, delicious in chai lattés or hot chocolates. It is a staple and we use it every day in the café — it is the only mylk we serve!

INGREDIENTS

1 cup (160g/5.6oz) **almonds**, soaked (see page 15)
5 **dates**
1 tsp **ground cinnamon**
½ tsp **sunflower lecithin**
4 cupes (1L) **filtered water**

METHOD

Place all ingredients in a high-speed blender and blend on high for 2–3 minutes until smooth. Place a nut mylk bag in a bowl and pour liquid into it. Strain the pulp by squeezing it through the bag until there is only hard pulp left. Pour mylk into a sealable jar and refrigerate. Mylk will be best in the first three days.

Makes 1L

TOMATO SAUCE

INGREDIENTS

5 large **tomatoes**
3 Tbsp **extra virgin olive oil**
1 Tbsp **coconut sugar**
½ **red capscium**
3 Tbsp **apple cider vinegar**
1 Tbsp **tamari**
1 tsp **salt**

METHOD

Cut the tomatoes into about 1cm wide slices and place on a dehydrator tray. Dehydrate for 4 hours. Place dehydrated tomatoes and remaining ingredients in a high-speed blender and blend until smooth. Store, refrigerated, in an airtight jar for up to one month.

Makes 2 cups

AIOLI

This aioli is a popular staple in my fridge and at the café. It is perfect for when you are looking for something to add a kick of flavour to a sandwich, a salad or a vegetable dish.

INGREDIENTS

2 cups (270g/9.6oz) **cashews**, soaked (see page 12)

⅓ cup (83ml) **filtered water**

1 clove **garlic**

1 tsp **Mustard** (see page 238)

3 Tbsp **lemon juice**

2 Tbsp **rice malt syrup**

1 tsp **Himalayan sea salt**

METHOD

Place all ingredients in a high-speed blender and blend until smooth, occasionally scraping down the sides to make sure all the ingredients are mixed in. Store, refrigerated, in an airtight jar for up to four weeks.

Makes 2½ cups

MANGO & GINGER CHUTNEY

I love this chutney on pizza bases, sandwiches, crackers and wraps.

INGREDIENTS

3 cups (300g/10.5oz) chopped **mango**

2 cups (320g/11.2oz) **dates**, soaked for 4 hours

1 small **shallot**, peeled and diced

⅓ cup (83ml) **apple cider vinegar**

1 tsp **Himalayan sea salt**

3cm **fresh ginger**

½ tsp **ground cloves**

METHOD

Place all ingredients in a food processor and process until smooth. Pour into a sterilised airtight jar and store, refrigerated, for up to two months.

Makes one 500ml jar

SAUERKRAUT

INGREDIENTS

1 red cabbage
3 Tbsp **Himalayan sea salt**

METHOD

Cut the cabbage into quarters and remove the core. Cut each quarter into 3cm wide strips. Place the cabbage and salt in a large bowl. Using your hands, massage the salt into the cabbage until it starts to soften, then add water to cover the cabbage. Place a plate on top and use a weight to hold it down. Leave for 2 hours.

Rinse the cabbage under cold water and drain. Pack cabbage into a sterilised 500ml airtight jar, leaving at least 2cm of space at the top. Seal the jar with the lid and let stand at room temperature for 5–10 days. After five days, try the Sauerkraut. Fermentation will have created a delicious tangy flavour. Store in the refrigerator and use within two months.

Makes one 500ml jar

PRESERVED LEMONS

INGREDIENTS

12 lemons
2 Tbsp Himalayan sea salt
4 cups (1L) extra virgin olive oil

METHOD

Wash eight lemons and trim the ends off. Rub the lemons with salt and place them in a 1L jar. Juice the four remaining lemons and use the juice to cover the salt-rubbed lemons. Seal the jar and set aside for one week.

Drain the lemon juice and fill the jar up with olive oil. This will further preserve the lemons and they will last up to six months. The lemons are ready to use after the first week, but the longer they are preserved, the more intense their flavour becomes.

MUSTARD

INGREDIENTS

½ cup (85g/3oz) yellow mustard seeds
1½ cups (375ml) filtered water
¾ cup (190ml) apple cider vinegar
1 cup (135g/4.8oz) cashews
½ cup (150g/5.3oz) rice malt syrup
½ tsp turmeric
½ tsp Himalayan sea salt

METHOD

Place mustard seeds in a bowl and soak in 3 cups of filtered water for 24 hours. Strain the mustard seeds and rinse in running water until water is clear. Make sure all 'jelly' is well rinsed off. Place the mustard seeds in a high-speed blender and add the remaining ingredients. Blend on medium for 3 minutes or until smooth. Store in an airtight jar for up to three months.

Makes 2 cups

PICKLED CUCUMBERS

INGREDIENTS

12 mini **cucumbers**

2 cups (500ml) **apple cider vinegar**

3 Tbsp **coconut sugar**

2 Tbsp **yellow mustard seeds**

1 Tbsp **fennel seeds**

1 tsp **salt**

METHOD

Place the cucumbers in a sterilised 1L airtight jar or two 500ml jars. Add the apple cider vinegar, coconut sugar, mustard seeds, fennel seeds and salt. Place the lid on the jar and give it a slight shake to mix the seeds. Refrigerate and let marinate for one week for the best flavour. Pickled Cucumbers will last up to three months. Refrigerate once opened.

Makes one 1L or two 500ml jars

PICKLED BEETROOT

INGREDIENTS

6 medium-sized **beetroots**

2 cups (500ml) **apple cider vinegar**

½ cup (100g/3.5oz) **coconut sugar**

1 tsp **salt**

1 Tbsp **olive oil**

METHOD

Peel the beetroots and slice into thin strips. Set aside. Place apple cider vinegar, coconut sugar, salt and olive oil in a high-speed blender and blend on medium for 1–2 minutes.

Stack the sliced beetroot into a sterilised 1L airtight jar or two 500ml jars, then pour in the blended pickling liquid, filling the jar up to the top. Refrigerate and let marinate for 24 hours before using. Pickled Beetroot will keep, refrigerated, for up to four weeks.

Makes one 1L or two 500ml jars

STRAWBERRY, CARDAMOM & PEPPER JAM

INGREDIENTS

3 cups (600g/21oz) chopped strawberries
1½ cups (375ml) filtered water
1 cup (300g/10.6oz) rice malt syrup
½ tsp vanilla bean powder
½ tsp cardamom seeds
pinch of freshly ground black pepper
½ tsp Himalayan sea salt
1 tsp guar gum

METHOD

Blend 2 cups of the strawberries with 1 cup of the filtered water in a high-speed blender. Add rice malt syrup, vanilla bean powder, cardamom seeds, pepper, sea salt and remaining water and blend again. Pour into a bowl and stir in the remaining strawberries. Mix in the guar gum and pour jam into a sterilised 1L airtight jar or several smaller jars. Store, refrigerated, for up to two months.

Makes one 1L jar

SPICED MARMALADE

INGREDIENTS

3 oranges
2 grapefruits
½ cup (150g/5.3oz) maple syrup
1 tsp vanilla
1 tsp cinnamon
5 star anises
½ tsp salt
1 tsp guar gum

METHOD

Peel the oranges and grapefruits and remove the white pith. Cut into very thin slices and then cut into quarters. Place in a bowl and stir in the remaining ingredients. Pour into a sterilised 500ml airtight jar. Store, refrigerated, for up to three months.

Makes one 500ml jar

VANILLA CASHEW YOGHURT

INGREDIENTS

2 cups (270g/9.6oz) **cashews**, soaked (see page 12)

1½ cups (375ml) **filtered water**

½ tsp **vanilla bean powder**

pinch of **Himalayan sea salt**

¼ cup (75g/2.6oz) **rice malt syrup** (optional)

1–2 **probiotic capsules**

½ cup (65g/2.3oz) **boysenberries**, to serve (optional)

METHOD

Place cashews, filtered water, vanilla bean powder, sea salt and rice malt syrup (optional) in a high-speed blender and blend on high until smooth. Add the contents of the probiotic capsule/s and briefly blend again to mix through. Pour into a glass container and place a tea towel over the top, fastened with a rubber band or a piece of string. Leave in a warm place (e.g. in a hot water cupboard or on top of a dehydrator or oven) to ferment for 12 hours. If you like a strong yoghurt taste then leave to ferment further and check again in another 12 hours.

When the yoghurt has reached your preferred taste, place a lid on top and refrigerate. It is best used within one week, as it will continue to ferment. I love to serve the yoghurt with boysenberries. Stir the berries into the yoghurt and let the colour seep through.

Makes one 500ml jar

TIP

I like to use vegan probiotic capsules, purchased from my local wholefood store. Alternatively, you can source great options on iherb.com. The more probiotic powder you use, the more tangy and stronger the yoghurt will be. I love a strong yoghurt, as I know that it is doing wonders for my digestive system; however, if you are new to making this yoghurt, I recommend starting with one capsule.

DETOXIFICATION

Eat food. Not too much. Mostly plants. – Michael Pollan

Detoxification is one of the most powerful steps you can take towards bettering your health and overall wellbeing. It is the key to kick-starting a new and improved you, boosting your natural energy levels and providing clarity and focus in your life.

All of us are born with the incredible power to heal ourselves. However, in our modern world it is easy to become over-burdened with toxins that place stress on these innate healing responses. Sugar, caffeine, alcohol, processed foods, stress and pollution can accumulate in the body and become too much for our elimination channels to handle.

Detoxification simply means assisting your body's natural detoxifying organs and processes by minimising your exposure to these harmful substances, while at the same time providing the correct and ultimate nourishment to your body. By getting rid of the bad and replacing it with the good you will enable these organs to work at their most optimal state, the state in which we are designed to live!

1-WEEK NOURISHING DETOX PLAN

There are many symptoms, both physical and emotional, one can experience that would suggest it may be time for a nourishing detox food plan. Fatigue, insomnia, headaches, anxiety, skin breakouts, bloating... the list goes on. These symptoms are telling you that it is time to make a change in your lifestyle.

This detox plan has been designed to encourage you to embrace real, healthy, healing foods for ultimate nourishment, to rest your digestive system and to take on board a brand-new attitude. Minimise your exposure to toxins and flood your body with the vitamins and minerals that are going to help you thrive! This plan includes a range of deliciously different raw meal, snack and drink options. It will provide your body with an abundance of live nutrients and enzymes and will leave you feeling energised, refreshed and focused.

DETOX PLAN

	Day 1	Day 2	Day 3	Day 4	Day 5
Upon rising	3 Tbsp apple cider vinegar and juice of 1 lemon in 300ml water	3 Tbsp apple cider vinegar and juice of 1 lemon in 300ml water	3 Tbsp apple cider vinegar and juice of 1 lemon in 300ml water	3 Tbsp apple cider vinegar and juice of 1 lemon in 300ml water	3 Tbsp apple cider vinegar and juice of 1 lemon in 300ml water
Breakfast	Green Alkaliser Smoothie	Bircher Muesli	Celebration of Greens Smoothie	Tropical Chia Pudding	Green Alkaliser Smoothie
Snack	Mint & Matcha Macaroons	Matcha Mylkshake	Pistachio & Rosemary Biscotti	Matcha Mylkshake	Passionfruit & Bee Pollen Macaroons
Lunch	Carrot, Coconut & Mint Salad	Carrot, Cumin & Coriander Soup	Collard Wrap	Mint, Edamame & Radish Salad	Onion Wrap
Snack	Strawberry & Cardamom jam on 1 slice of Sprouted Buckwheat Loaf	Kale Chips	Piece of fruit with Vanilla Cashew Yoghurt	Black Sesame Crackers with Rosemary Oregano Pesto	Kale Chips
Dinner	Carrot Fettucine	Strawberry, Watercress & Almond Feta Salad	North African Salad	Massaman Curry with Coconut Rice	Beetroot Risotto with Wasabi Cream
After dinner	Strawberry & Mint Kefir	Peach & Lavender Ice Tea	Chamomile Choc Mylk	Ginger & Rose Kombucha	Mayan Hot Chocolate

INDEX

ACKNOWLEDGEMENTS

Firstly, I would like to thank the Universe for making this cookbook possible. Raw food really is my pure passion and it is a blessing to be able to express my love and creativity in a book for others to enjoy.

My heartfelt thanks to all the following people:

My partner Joss for always believing in me, supporting me and putting up with my crazy ideas!

My parents for always being that little bit more creative in the kitchen, and for setting a great example of wholesome eating and how to eat as a family.

Granny Ann for showing me a world greater than us and for inspiring my interest in food energy and herbal remedies.

The wonderful team at The Raw Kitchen. Each and every one of you has contributed to the journey of The Raw Kitchen in your endless positivity and passion.

Nutritionist Annabel Roydhouse for the detox-plan development.

Recipe tester Aimee Short.

A huge thank you to Sally and the excellent team at Beatnik Publishing. It has been a pleasure working with such a fun and hands-on team.

NEST and Steiner Ceramics for props, and Ruby for costume.

Lastly, all the customers of The Raw Kitchen. Without you, none of this would have been possible.

Olivia. S

OLIVIA SCOTT